Romans

A Novel

Alice Birch

methuen | drama

LONDON · NEW YORK · OXFORD · NEW DELHI · SYDNEY

METHUEN DRAMA
Bloomsbury Publishing Plc, 50 Bedford Square, London, WC1B 3DP, UK
Bloomsbury Publishing Inc, 1359 Broadway, New York, NY 10018, USA
Bloomsbury Publishing Ireland, 29 Earlsfort Terrace, Dublin 2,
D02 AY28, Ireland

BLOOMSBURY, METHUEN DRAMA and the Methuen
Drama logo are trademarks of Bloomsbury Publishing Plc.

First published in Great Britain 2025

Cover image: Kyle Soller photographed by Nadav Kander

A catalogue record for this book is available from the British Library.

Library of Congress Control Number: 2025945583

ISBN: PB: 978-1-3506-0553-4
ePDF: 978-1-3506-0554-1
eBook: 978-1-3506-0555-8

Series: Modern Plays

Typeset by Mark Heslington Ltd, Scarborough, North Yorkshire
Printed and bound in Great Britain

For product safety related questions contact
productsafety@bloomsbury.com.

To find out more about our authors and books visit
www.bloomsbury.com and sign up for our newsletters.

ROMANS
A NOVEL

By **Alice Birch**

Directed by **Sam Pritchard**

9 September–11 October 2025

CAST

John/Henry/Charles/Manolin/ Clifford/Benny/Patrick/Thomas	**Declan Conlon**
Rosa/Anna/Waitress	**Yanexi Enriquez**
Emilio/Bernard/Officer/Timothy/ Joe/Tommy	**Olivier Huband**
Marlow	**Oliver Johnstone**
Poole/Ramsay/Leo/Prufrock/ James/Johnny	**Jerry Killick**
Esther/Marianne	**Adelle Leonce**
Clarissa/Lucy/Miranda	**Agnes O'Casey**
Jack	**Kyle Soller**
Edmund	**Stuart Thompson**

CREATIVE TEAM

Writer	**Alice Birch**
Director	**Sam Pritchard**
Set and Costume Designer	**Merle Hensel**
Lighting Designer	**Lee Curran**
Sound Designer	**Benjamin Grant**
Composer	**Jasmin Kent Rodgman**
Movement Director	**Hannes Langolf**
Casting Director	**Amy Ball CDG**
Costume Supervisor	**Jackie Orton**
Wigs, Hair and Makeup Supervisor	**Sophia Khan**
Fight Director	**Bret Yount**
Vocal Coach	**Michaela Kennen**
Assistant Director	**Neetu Singh**

ALMEIDA THEATRE

About the Almeida:

Since 2013, the Almeida has been led by Artistic Director Rupert Goold and Executive Director Denise Wood (Dominic Cooke will take over as Artistic Director in 2025). During their tenure, notable productions have included *American Psycho: a new musical thriller* (transferred to Broadway); *Chimerica* (transferred to the West End and won five Olivier Awards); *1984* (transferred to the West End, Broadway and Australia); *King Charles III* (transferred to the West End, won the Olivier Award for Best New Play, transferred to Broadway, toured the UK and Sydney, and was adapted for BBC television); *Oresteia* and *Hamlet* (both transferred to Park Avenue Armory, New York after successful West End runs); *Mary Stuart* (transferred to the West End and toured the UK); *Summer and Smoke* (transferred to the West End and won two Olivier Awards including Best Revival); and *The Hunt* (transferred to St. Ann's Warehouse, New York). Recent highlights include *The Years* (transferred to the West End, winner of two Olivier Awards), *A Streetcar Named Desire* (won three Olivier Awards including Best Revival; returned to the West End this year followed by a run at Brooklyn Academy of Music), *Patriots* (transferred to the West End and Broadway) and *The Doctor* (transferred to the West End and Park Avenue Armory, New York), as well as critically acclaimed productions of *Spring Awakening* (screened in cinemas UK wide), *The Tragedy of Macbeth* (screened on BBC Four and available on BBC iPlayer) and *Tammy Faye* (ran on Broadway last year).

The Almeida Theatre is a registered charity and is dependent on the support of individuals, companies and trusts and foundations to realise our artistic ambitions, nurture emerging talent and connect with over 4,000 young people and community each year through Almeida

Participation. We gratefully acknowledge the generosity of our supporters.

The Almeida is grateful for the support of Arts Council England.

SAM PRITCHARD
Director

Sam is a theatre director working across the UK and internationally. He was an Associate Director at the Royal Court between 2016 and 2024, where he also ran the theatre's International Programme working with writers across the world. Sam began his career as the New Writing Associate at the Royal Exchange Theatre, Manchester and won the JMK Award for Directors in 2012.

Theatre includes: *all of it* (Royal Court/Festival d'Avignon); *A Fight Against... (Una Lucha Contra...)* (Royal Court/Santiago a Mil); *The Mysteries* (Royal Exchange Theatre, Manchester/ UK tour); *Mates in Chelsea, Pity, Grimly Handsome, B* (Royal Court); *Pygmalion* (Headlong/Leeds Playhouse/Nuffield Southampton Theatres/UK tour); *There Has Possibly Been an Incident* (Royal Exchange Theatre, Manchester/Soho Theatre/Edinburgh Festival Fringe/Theatertreffen, Berlin); *Fireface* (Young Vic); *Galka Motalka* (Royal Exchange Theatre, Manchester).

ALICE BIRCH
Writer

Theatre includes: *The House of Bernarda Alba* (National Theatre); *Orlando* (Schaubühne, Berlin); *[BLANK]* (Donmar Warehouse); *Anatomy of a Suicide* (Royal Court, winner of the Susan Smith Blackburn Prize); *Revolt. She Said. Revolt Again.* (RSC, co-winner of the George Devine Award); *Ophelias Zimmer* (Royal Court/ Schaubühne, Berlin).

Film includes: *Die, My Love* (co-written with Lynne Ramsay and Enda Walsh); *The End We Start From*; *The Wonder* (co-written with Sebastián Lelio and Emma Donoghue); *Mothering Sunday*; *Lady Macbeth* (BIFA for Best Screenplay and BAFTA nomination for Outstanding Debut).

Television includes: *Dead Ringers* (winner of the Peabody Award); *Normal People* (Emmy Award nomination for Outstanding Writing for a Limited Series); *Conversations with Friends*; *Succession* (Story Editor for season two).

Thanks to: Rupert Goold and Steph Bain for all of their extraordinary support and faith. To everyone at the Almeida – to Sam South and Rebecca Frecknall, and to Declan, Yanexi, Olivier, Oliver, Jerry, Adelle, Agnes, Stuart and Kyle for taking such brilliant care of the words, characters, ideas and for making them bigger. To the whole creative team: Merle, Lee, Hannes, Benjamin, Jasmine, Amy, Jackie, Sophia, Neetu, Beth, Catt, Daiva, Luanne, and to Emily and the production team. Thanks to Giles, Lee, Geoff and Rachel. Thanks to Hilton Als, to Tessa Ross for being early readers. Thank you Sam, for everything and for all of it. And to Sorrel and Arthur, always.

Romans

/ Denotes the overlapping of speech.

Words in square brackets [ ] are not spoken.

The absence of a full stop at the end of a line denotes a kind
of interruption – the lines should run at speed.

The use of a full stop on a line on its own denotes a pause.

The spacing of the dialogue, the use of upper and lower case
letters and the punctuation is all there to help the actor in
terms of the pacing and the weight of their words.

Part One

WINTER

One

Jack   My father wanted only sons but he had to get through four dead daughters before he got to the sons, but at least the sons lived.

.

It wasn't Cruel, this Want. It wasn't anything to do with not *liking* girls – it didn't share the same Air as that notion – my father was many things but he was not so silly as to engage with *like* or *DisLike* – he felt life was for grabbing at the edges – Opera only, Passion or Despair. It had nothing to do with not Enjoying the company of women – Quite the contrary, my father took great pleasure in the delights that only the female presence can provide – never was a man more devoted to his wife than my Father to my Mother – indeed, his Wanting sons was entirely that – a Want, a desire, an Exertion *InTo* the world rather than a Lack, a Fear, a Void. He *Wanted* boys, he Wanted masculinity, jaws, fists, violence, speed, drive, money, virility, opportunity, spit and testicles, tyranny, two feet hip width apart, bullets, mud, straight backed, dirt and rolling with the dogs on a wooden floor.

Two

A field near a large country house. It's barren, wild, overgrown. Fog.

It's early evening in late winter – it's beginning to get dark. It's been a bright, cold day with no wind. Breath forms in clouds.

Jack *(age ten) has been walking across the fields, back towards home. Or, at least, he was. In front of him stands **John**. Dressed in some sort of military uniform. Relatively high ranking, but he's been on a battlefield. It used to fit him but now it hangs off his body. He's covered in mud and dried blood. He has a gun – a breech-loading shot rifle with a long sword bayonet – on his back.*

John   And through the fog there is a man.

.

Hello.

.

Jack   Sir.

John   .

You must be John.

Jack   My name is Jack, sir.

John   Ah.

.

I wanted to be a Jack but my Mother didn't like it.

Jack   Mine does. She says it suits me. She says that I am CareFree.

John   That is surely the best way for a young man To be

Jack   It wouldn't suit you. You look like you have cares.

John   .

Some.

.

Do you know my name.

Jack   You are Uncle John.

You have been at war.

You have killed lots of people.

You have been very brave but now you are broken, Mother says.

.

I pretend to be you when I play with my brother Marlow. I poke him with a butter knife and he cries.

He is just a baby.

Mother says I am to use a spoon from now on.

John   .

And how is your father?

Jack   Very well, sir.

Business is Thriving.

Business is Positively Booming.

At least, that's what he says to the men who come to the factory or sometimes to dinner at our house. At night I hear him crying and Mother saying sssshhh and that there is nothing to be Ashamed of – a Man crying in his own home in the small hours on account of the Burden of providing for his family is a very Noble thing.

John   .

Well. Your Mother always was terribly Forgiving.

Jack   .

Why doesn't he have a Gun, like you.

John   Men are different

Jack   Father owns a printing press

John   Yes

Jack   Not a gun, but a Printing Press

John   Yes

Jack   It's very important work

Nothing is of higher value to man than the Integrity of the Written Word.

John   Is that so.

Jack   What my Father does is very *Noble* – I have just learnt that word

John   I am not sure you have.

Jack   .

I don't want anything to do with it, I think Printing Presses are exceedingly boring.

John   .

What do you like doing if you don't like Printing Presses, Jack.

Jack   Fishing. Climbing. Catching rabbits.

.

John   And your Mother, how is she?

Jack   Having a baby, sir.

I've been sent away from the house on account of all the screaming.

.

John   Will she survive.

Jack   What a stupid question

John   It is?

Jack   Of course she will survive, she is my Mother

John   Yes

Jack   Sometimes the babies die but never Mother

John   I see

Jack   You are a stupid man

John   And I could cut your fucking head off.

.

Jack   That's our house just there. The red brick – do you
see it

John   I do

Jack   The one with all the ivy and the jasmine around the
door

John   Yes

Jack   It's very grand, is it not

John   It is

Jack   We have horses and several fireplaces and eight
bedrooms

John   I see

Jack   Four servants and a Rather handsome library

John   I have been sleeping under the stars and digging the
earth near trees – oak and beech and ash and sycamore.

Jack   .

Father is a SelfMade Man

John   What man isn't.

.

It does not look like the house We grew up in.

Jack   No, well that was hovel, says Father.

John   Does he indeed

Jack   Indeed He Does, sir

John   .

This was your Mother's house. As a girl.

Jack   Yes.

John   He always said he'd have it.

Jack   .

Are you hurt.

Are you wounded, sir

John   Not presently

Jack   Then why are you covered in blood

John   The blood is not my own

Jack   Did you kill someone

John   Many people

Jack   With that gun

John   Yes

Jack   May I hold it

John   If you like.

He gives **Jack** *the gun.* **Jack** *is thrilled. He raises it. Spins around with it. Points it at* **John** *who stands upright in front of him.*

John   Good.

Jack *lowers it.*

John   Up.

Jack *hesitates.*

John   UP.

Jack *raises it.*

John   My heart.

Jack *points it at his heart.*

John   Good.

Now my head.

Jack *raises it to his head.*

John   Steady. Good.

.

Now pull the trigger.

Jack *immediately lowers the gun.*

John   Pull it.

Jack *stares at him.*

John   Lift the gun LIFT IT –

he does –

and **John** *walks towards him, seizing the barrel of the gun and pushing it into his stomach,* **Jack** *trying to pull it back, upset, until* **John** *wrenches it from him, shouting 'BANG' as he does –*

John   See!

Wasn't that fun Your heart is racing

Your Blood is pumping

You are running on instinct, nerves, feelings – All Thought Gone – and Now *You* are Upright, *You* are standing and another man is dead and on the ground – *this* is what it means to be truly alive, Jack – you cannot simply Live, it must be Claimed Constantly, living and staring at death in another's face – then, Then, you are a man upon this earth.

Jack *stares at him.* **John** *is out of breath. Steadying himself.* **Jack** *is half horrified, half thrilled.*

.

Jack   Have you come home.

John   .

This is not my home.

.

I went to war and everybody died. My Father, my Mother, my sister?

Jack   Yes, sir.

They all took such a long time. Grandfather couldn't stop wailing.

John   Men cry and scream in houses at night it seems. Perhaps that is what happens when a war is on.

Perhaps death spreads into the cracks in the walls and the floorboards. Punishment because none of you are at war.

Or, perhaps, Death is simply collecting the bodies owed to him in answer to our

cowardly prayers.

not me. don't let me die. not me. take somebody else. anybody else.

.

Jack   You didn't say that.

.

John   No.

But I thought it.

Jack   .

You look very hungry, sir.

John   I believe I am, I have forgotten what the beginning of hunger feels like. I am used to the moment that follows. The agony. The pleasure.

.

Jack   Will you come back to the house.

Mary will make you something.

Mary is our cook.

She looked after you as a baby, she is spectacularly old.

John   An oak tree.

Jack   Yes, sir

John   I do not remember her.

I do not remember much. I remember your Mother.

Perhaps you might bring me something

Jack   Anything

John   In the event that they not so happy to see me

Jack   I believe that they are sad that you are gone away so long and that you do not write.

I can't wait to leave.

John   You're unhappy?

Jack   No, sir, I am very happy – I have had a childhood Without Blemish, Mother says

John   Yes, I believe that to be the case

Jack   I just plan on having the Most Adventurous life and that must be done Away from here

John   Yes. Yes, I can see that it must.

Where will you go.

Jack   I like the books about Men At Sea.

John   Yes.

Jack   And on Mountains and at War.

John   I see.

Jack   And then I will come home.

I will come home often. Mother will miss me so terribly if I do not.

John   .

Sometimes it is hard to come home following adventures. Depending on what they are.

Depending on what you have done. They might turn you into an animal. Or made of glass.

They might cover you in candlelight. Or black oil.

If I come home they will see what I Am now, on my face, they will smell it on my breath, they will feel it at my touch – even if I try to conceal it – see –

he grins

it drops

they will find it, they will squirrel it out and besides – I do not know how to Be in a drawing room or a library or a ballroom or in the arms of another or reflected in the eyes of someone who has goodness in their soul – because I am This now, muscles and sinew, organs and tissue, blood and spit and I wouldn't Want to be what I was before because it would not be the Truth, Jack.

So much Blemish.

.

You are right to seek adventure. You are right to hold it as the Highest importance. Adventure and Truth. Sacrifice everything for it. It is worth it. I promise. Terror and Joy.

.

He barks.

Jack *doesn't jump.*

Jack *whistles. Clicks his fingers. Looks at* **John**.

Jack   Here, boy.

John *stares.*

In the distance, shouting from the house. People shouting **Jack**'s *name.* **Jack** *keeps looking at* **John**.

Jack   I will bring you some food and something to drink, and some clean clothes. And then you will come home and everyone will embrace you. Father will cry. Mother too.

And the babies, but that's just because they are babies. You and I will remain calm, that will be Important, that the two of us are very Calm, we will Reassure everyone that everything will be fine now, it might be strange for a little while, but then everything will find its place and you will be happy here with us again and you can tell us the stories of war. The terror and the joy.

Uncle John.

You can come Inside. You can come home.

.

Jack *leaves.* **John** *watches him go.*

Three

Jack   Nobody believed that I had seen my Uncle – the Lieutenant John James Roman that afternoon. He had been gone for so many years, and had ceased all correspondence for the last two that Father had all but declared him dead, and his existence in our lives had been exiled to a strange, liminal space.

He crept like a ghost around my father's features – the mention of his name would pull a smile, a reflex of deep childhood joy – memories of playing in streams, attics, muddy fields and a schoolroom together. This would be followed by grief or anger, depending on the amount of drink he had in him, or the proximity of the men he did business with, who were increasingly losing patience, or, more damagingly – faith. John was neither allowed to be alive nor deceased, hoped for or remembered, a memory nor a tomorrow.

I returned from the fields that day full of stolen glory. I felt as though *I* had been the soldier upon the battlefield, that *I* were the one whose clothes were soaked in the blood of another man. I barely touched my supper, and then raided the kitchen, taking bread and chicken, ham and grapes from a clucking Mary, who loved me too much to scold on an ordinary day, let alone a day when the house seemed to be being subsumed with a slow, mouth-gaping panic that I was too busy and important to notice or take seriously. It was as though grief and horror was slowly being pumped beneath the doors and through the chimneys and in cracks where we had forgotten to close the windows. I was giddy. I couldn't see it.

I left the house – and my mother's full-throated screams – and ran back to the fields, calling his name, whistling and slapping my thigh, half expecting him to bound towards me on all fours like one of our labs.

I roamed the fields and the nearby woods for hours. I kept on shouting his name, shouting until my voice was almost gone and I found myself back at the house where I had a new baby brother – Edmund – and a dead mother.

.

The snow came in that night, pushing the crocuses back into their sleep and Uncle John back into that passage of nothing between time and space. The more I insisted that I Had seen him, met him, spoke with him, made Promises to him, the angrier my until then relatively sweet and placid Father became.

I couldn't seem to hear the words that Mother had died.

Nor could I hear the sounds of Marlow wailing for her, held by Mary, her own cries a soprano accompaniment, I was so intent on making Father understand that Uncle John was alive, was lost in the woods or the fields perhaps – as though if he were to accept *that* then perhaps his wife would still be living and this new baby – Edmund, Marlow and I not suddenly, catastrophically Motherless.

In the weeks that followed we buried my Mother beneath six feet of dirt and a sheet of ice and Father disappeared in a fog of grief. I spent the days roaming the fields, the woods, the lanes, the ditches, the brooks, the hills, the valleys, the rivers, the bracken, the lakes, the earth for John.

A month after my Mother had gone to God, my Father sent me to boarding school. Though his debts were increasing and his ability to work profitably appeared to be vanishing, my Mother's parents offered the school fees and he gladly accepted.

So. Off I went. By train, by carriage, by foot to the high walls of Cowan School and the cold brutality of Mr Poole.

Four

Night. The cricket pitch of a school. **Jack** *is seventeen. Standing next to* **Jack** *is* **Marlow**. *He is ten. They are both in uniformed pyjamas.* **Marlow** *has wet himself. He has been crying but is trying to stop.* **Poole** *stands opposite them. There is snow on the ground. They are all wearing shoes.*

Poole   Jack Roman, where are we standing.

Jack   On the cricket pitch, sir.

Poole   On the grounds of.

Jack   Cowan School, sir.

Poole   And is Cowan School a school for girls or for boys, Roman?

Jack   It is a school for boys, sir.

Poole   Then why am I looking at two little girls.

Jack   .

Poole   I asked you a question

Jack   You are not, sir.

We are boys, sir.

We are brothers. And we are boys. Sir.

.

Poole   What is your age.

Jack   Seventeen, sir.

Poole   Not seven.

Jack   No, sir.

Poole   .

And you.

How many years have you.

Marlow .

I am ten, sir.

Poole You are Motherless, are you not?

Jack Our Mother died when I was ten and Marlow was just three, sir.

Poole .

Did she smother you, your mother, was she a Smotherer.

Jack .

She was a very loving Mother, sir. I miss her very much. I am very proud to be her son

Poole *slaps him. He doesn't flinch.* **Marlow** *does.*

Poole And your Father.

Jack .

Yes, sir.

Poole You are proud to be his son.

Jack .

Yes, sir

Poole You hesitate

Jack No, sir

Poole Your Father is an insolvent drunk, frequently seen weeping in the street.

Jack .

Poole Will you not Defend him

Jack My Father has had his struggles, but what man Has not. And, sir, he is Decent and he is Kind, despite his hardships and I believe that to be Honourable

Poole Do you know what the word Honourable means

Jack   I believe so, sir

Poole *hits him again. He does not flinch.* **Marlow** *does.*

.

Remove your shoes and your socks, your shirt and your trousers.

Jack   .

Slowly, he does. He folds his clothes neatly. He stands, barefoot on the snow. It is painful. He tries very hard to contain it. **Marlow** *looks panicked, upset.* **Poole** *removes his belt.* **Jack***'s body is covered in scars where he has been thrashed with a belt or a cane.*

Poole   Is it cold

Jack   Yes, sir

Poole   Does it burn

Jack   Yes, sir

Poole   Assume your position.

Jack *bends his knees. Holds his arms out straight in front of him. It's a stress position.*

Do you remember your brother before he left home?

Marlow   not very well, sir.

Poole   You were three.

Marlow   yes, sir.

Poole   And your Mother had just died.

Marlow   yes, sir.

Poole   A difficult time for any young girl.

Marlow   .

I am a boy, sir

Poole *thrashes* **Marlow** *with the belt, this makes* **Jack** *almost topple over in shock and protest – which makes* **Poole** *strike* **Marlow** *again, who screams -*

Jack   Sir

Poole (*striking* **Marlow**, *speaking to* **Jack**)   Every time you Move, I will strike him

Jack   Sir, please

Poole (*striking* **Marlow**)   Every time you Speak without being Spoken To, I will strike him

Jack   Hit me instead, sir, please

Poole (*striking* **Marlow**)   You Move, I hit him, You Speak without invitation, I strike him, do you understand?

Jack   .

Poole (*striking* **Marlow**)   Do You / Under*stand*

Jack   / Yes, sir, yes.

.

Marlow *is sobbing.* **Jack** *is managing not to.*

Poole   You wet the bed.

Marlow   Yes, sir, I did, sir, I am sorry, sir.

Poole   You have been here one week

Marlow   Yes, sir

Poole   And you have wet the bed every single night.

Marlow   I am sorry, sir, I do not know how to control it.

Poole   It would appear not.

You sleep in soiled sheets.

Marlow   Mr Brooks says I may not change them until I learn not to do it, sir.

Poole   A sensible idea.

Marlow   Yes, sir.

Poole   It runs in the family.

Marlow   .

Sir.

Poole   Jack.

Jack   Sir.

Poole   What happened your first week at Cowan.

Jack   I wet the bed every night, sir.

Poole   And then.

Jack   .

.

Poole   And

Then

Jack   I stopped

Poole   Because.

Jack   .

.

Poole *strikes* **Marlow,** *who sobs,* **Jack** *flinches, he strikes him again*

Poole   Because

Jack   no

The violence is repeated.

Poole   Because

Jack   I

The violence is repeated.

Poole   Because

Jack   no

Poole   Tell the Truth

Jack   I

The violence is repeated.

Poole   Because

Jack   I

The violence is repeated.

Poole   Because

Jack   I can't.

A pause. **Marlow** *looks horrified. Stares at his brother.*

Poole   Very good.

.

(*To* **Marlow**.) Follow me.

Jack   .

Sir

please don't.

please. take me instead.

.

Poole   Proverbs 13, 24.

Jack   .

Poole   Proverbs 13, 24.

Jack   .

Whoever spares the rod hates his son. But he who loves him
is diligent to discipline him.

Poole   Where is my office.

Jack   Over there, sir.

Poole   What does it overlook.

Jack   .

The cricket pitch, sir.

Poole   You are to stay here.

You will be able to listen from here if your brother has anything like the lungs you have.

I will watch you from the window. Move, and I will make it worse for him. Understood?

.

Jack *nods.*

.

Jack (*to* **Marlow**)   it will end. it does end.

Marlow *and* **Poole** *leave.*

.

Time passes.

.

Birdsong.

Jack *turns his head, slightly.*

From offstage, **Marlow** *screams.*

Five

Jack   Marlow never wet the bed ever again. He also refused to speak to me for three and a half months and when he did find the words they were usually insults.

How quickly he became cruel. I felt Floored by it.

Marlow had been a sweet, soft, sensitive child, round cheeks and freckles, big eyes and long lashes. He looked more like Mother than Edmund or I did, and so perhaps for a while we treated him as though he Was her, needing him, coddling him, grateful for some continuation of her, failing to Meet him as he was – and, of course, it turned out that he was the least like her of / the three of us

Marlow   / that isn't true.

Jack   .

He couldn't forgive me. Decided that it was My doing that he was led into that awful room and presumably endured what I had had to endure seven years earlier.

Perhaps if I had described it, that would have been humiliation enough and Marlow would have been spared – the horror of that haunted me and fuelled his fury. When I had the *Audacity* to ask what had happened, why he had screamed, he Spat at me – *How Dare You* and I could see his point. How *Dare* I when I hadn't dared that night. Somehow Mr Poole became blameless and Marlow quickly did well at school, became a favourite of the teachers, turned out to have an instinctive, delicious flair for sadism. He became Head Boy. Took pleasure in beating the younger ones. If violence is being inflicted upon somebody else then it Isn't being directed at you.

He'd have them stand in impossible positions on the cricket pitch and watch over them with Poole's belt looped around his own skinny wrist – he had found his Calling, found what he was good at Found how to Excel, Found how to make others proud of him, how to make them laugh and clap their hands together with surprise and joy – Clever you, Clever boy – he had found that what he was better than anybody else at was Cruelty.

I finished school in a paler hue – already my teachers frowning slightly, trying to recollect Who on earth I was, or what I had achieved or summon any significant memory of me pertaining to an Achievement or even Failure – but nothing, I had failed to make an impact beyond being the older, less impressive brother of Marlow Roman.

.

Letters from home hurried towards me; there was yet time to step into the family business and resurrect its corpse, its death rattle not yet audible to investors and clients – but what I wanted.

What I Wanted.

.

A new war was rolling in across Europe and bombs were falling on cities. Quick and decisive in war rooms and stumbling and gasping on the field, I was keen to be a part of it, be in the thick of it, feel my elbows sharp against another, my forearms soft against another, convinced that if I was in amongst it all I might find my meaning, might find Uncle John, might find myself, adrenaline, thrill and truth and terror and joy.

Six

A dark room in **Jack***'s childhood home. Candlelight.* **Jack** *is standing.* **Henry** *sits at the head of a long table. A plate of food in front of him. A glass of wine and a bottle. A plate of food at the other end of the table intended for* **Jack**. **Henry** *is hunched over his chair, his hair white. He is close to fifty, but he looks eighty.* **Jack** *is twenty. He is wearing a military uniform. He has a gun.*

The house is crumbling. Damp is crawling from floor to ceiling. In one corner of the room, water drips into a bucket. In another, it drips onto the floor. **Henry** *is drunk.* **Jack** *is sober.*

Henry The Prodigal returns.

The Bloody Soldier.

Jack   .

Father.

Henry   Come home at last

Jack   Sir

Henry   How good of you to grace us with your presence.

Jack   .

Henry   Step into the light then, let us have a look at you, further, a little further, you are a blur.

.

Goodness.

How you Glitter. Don't you *Sparkle.*

How many lives did you stop in order to have so many Jewels draped upon you

Jack   Too many to count

Henry   Said with such a serious expression

Jack   It is a serious thing

Henry   No fun had at all

Jack   No, sir, I wouldn't describe it as Fun

Henry   But it was what you Wanted

Jack   Yes

Henry   You Wanted to go to battle and so you did

Jack   Yes

Henry   Then what is the fucking problem.

.

Put your gun down.

.

Put it Down, I will not have you standing in my house with a Gun on your body and your face full of misery.

Jack *puts the gun on the table.*

Jack   What has happened to the house

Henry   What has Happened to it

Jack   Yes, sir

Henry   Is it not Grand enough for you

Jack   It is falling apart

Henry   Was I to string up some decorations, gather some flowers, assemble the villagers and sing you a song

Jack   You have let it go to ruin.

Henry   I have *let it.*

Jack   Either that or you have done it with Purpose.

Henry   Ah.

Jack   Broken it because of your own misery.

Henry   Goodness, haven't you Grown.

And you.

Jack   Sir

Henry   Are you broken because of what you have failed to attend to or are you ruining yourself with purpose.

Jack   I am not.

You Left Me

Jack   You sent me away

Henry   And then I sent for your return – you are my firstborn, it is your Duty to come home

Jack   There was a war, sir

Henry   Oh there was a War was there there was a fucking War was there there were Men to be murdered and countries to be Conquered

Jack   You have never Been to war, sir, you do not know what it is like.

Henry   I have been to war.

Jack   For three days.

Henry   I should have pulled the shrapnel from my leg with my bare hands and continued firing

Jack   I have seen men do just that

Henry   And for what

Jack   For Honour

Henry   And what is Honour

Jack   For King and for country

Henry   You say words but you do not say anything that has any Meaning you are a Parrot Sit down.

Jack   I am proud of what I have done

Henry   You are a liar you have ripped out your soul for Nothing, cannon fodder for someone else's purpose and you will not even question it

Jack   The words a coward uses to comfort himself where is Edmund

Henry   You are In my house Sit Down.

Jack *sits*.

Henry   So we are a great disappointment to one another.

Jack   Why didn't you write and Tell me how bad things had gotten.

Henry   Why didn't You

Jack   I did.

Many times.

Henry   I stopped reading your letters.

Jack   .

Where is Edmund.

Henry   You know who writes an Excellent letter

Jack   I do not

Henry   Marlow

Jack   Ah

Henry   Most entertaining

Jack   Glad to hear you are being entertained

Henry   He *Knows* himself

Jack   Does he

Henry   He has Arrived at himself Fully Formed, he understands his weaknesses and his flaws, he is engaged in self-improvement but not apology – your words were full of regret and complaint and bitterness and grandeur – it was like reading your Uncle's letters years ago

Jack   Whilst I am sorry that you did not Enjoy them I take that as a compliment, sir.

Henry   Do not Call me sir and sit at my table and eat my bread whilst there is a Sneer UpOn your face you are so like him

Jack   You intend to insult yet I receive it as Praise

Henry   You hold him in such regard and yet you never knew him

Jack   I met him the night Mother died. On the fields. I have told you.

Henry   You are a liar.

Jack   I have many failings but I am not a liar.

Henry   You know that I stole her from him.

As **Henry** *speaks,* **Edmund** *enters, soft, quiet, unnoticed. He's ten. He's wearing what is clearly his Mother's dress.*

Henry   We grew up together.

John and I in the farmhouse at the end of the lane, and your Mother in this beautiful house at the top of the hill. We had enough, we were Loved, but there was no silverware, no silks, and your Mother's parents used to throw these parties once a month. Women wearing lemon and lavender coloured gowns and emeralds and diamonds on collarbones, draped over wrists and bony fingers. There were eclairs and jellies, sandwiches and ice creams on the lawn, we'd play cricket and hide and seek and we'd climb these magnificent oak trees and swim in the lake and lie out on the grass under the sun and your Mother liked my Brother John better than anybody. He climbed higher than the other boys.

He jumped into the water in December and didn't shriek.

He shot foxes and rode horses and smoked cigarettes and when her dog died he dug the grave and pulled her hair back with his fingers thick with mud and he only spoke when he Had to and he touched the small of her back and her arms and when he thought nobody was looking he pressed himself against her and bit her ear and laid his palm flat against her chest and Moved.

He climbed the walls.

He hid in the stables.

He pinned her to the wall with a look like a spider and he promised her that there would never be another and when the bullet hit my leg I knew that that was my opportunity to take it all from him and I was Queasy with joy.

She was a Good Nurse and I was a Good Patient and it took surprisingly little to persuade her that John thought nothing of her, not really.

She never loved me as she loved him. But I didn't care.

I had her.

I had her for her whole life. I had her and he didn't.

.

Jack   Am I yours.

Henry *smiles.*

Henry   .

I never did know.

.

I never had to think about it.

He was gone and then You were gone and. I didn't have to look at you.

At your face.

Which may as well be His face.

.

It was as though it had all happened an entirely different way.

.

Ah.

Look now.

Look who has come home to join us, my love.

Jack *turns and notices* **Edmund** *for the first time. He is appalled.*

Henry   Boy can barely speak, he's so moved.

Jack   Edmund

Henry   Not Edmund, we don't use that name

Jack   What have you Done to him

Henry   What has Happened to the house what have you Done to him you sound Deranged

Jack   Look at him

Henry   Unhinged

Jack   Look At Him

Henry   Who Are you, why are you Here?

.

We decided Edmund had died a little while ago did we not

Edmund   we did

Henry   We found it made us both happier, did it not

Edmund   it did

Jack   .

I am not yours. I cannot be.

.

After a moment, **Henry** *picks up the gun.*

A beat.

Jack   Father –

Henry   No.

No.

Not I.

He raises it to his head and we cut to black.

Part Two

SPRING

*Movement. There are three men, in three separate places – **Jack**, **Marlow** and **Edmund**. They are all on the move. They do not speak to each other, they are in their own places, though sometimes they are writing letters to one another, and then occasionally – when it is obvious – they are in dialogue with one another. Maybe it's a revolve – motion is important. At the start of this, **Jack** is twenty-seven, **Marlow** is twenty, **Edmund** is seventeen.*

Edmund   Dearest Jack, please come back and get me.

Jack   I have never seen the mountains before.

Edmund   Dear Marlow, please come and fetch me.

Marlow   We have found the trees that Weep.

Ramsay   Hello

Jack   Hello

Ramsay   He has the face and structure of every man who has lived through the War – more child than man, but endured more than any man ought to – all shoulders and soft skin, trembling hands and a step that treads before he has allowed himself to consider any caution but then the mountains draw Romantics and Fools – Keep Pace

Jack   Mm

Ramsay   You are unwell?

Jack   The Third Man

Ramsay   Ah

Jack   The spirit that guides lost men on mountains

Ramsay   You are not lost, follow my boots

Jack   Spoken like a good spirit

Ramsay   You may grip my hand and see

Jack   Yes

Ramsay   That I am quite real

Jack   A spirit would convince me of its presence by taking a corporeal form

Ramsay   Perhaps

Marlow   We travelled along the river through thick oppressive jungle that I can barely begin to describe, in a heat that the English language has not sufficient words for, my skin heavy with a slow, damp sweat that the locals do not endure

Edmund   Dearest Jack, I have left the Caraways. I am sorry about that, because I know you wanted me to stay there, but truthfully, they did not seem to enjoy my company, and I feel, perhaps, I hope, perhaps that there might be somewhere I am wanted more.

Marlow   We have seen sloths and spider monkeys, macaws and toucans, snakes of a hundred different varieties and jaguars. It is hard to believe that we are on the same planet as where we began our journeys but God is Almighty.

Jack   On the descent, a man slipped

Ramsay   PULL

Jack   He was holding the rope and the two men beneath him naturally slipped also

Ramsay   PULL

Jack   The rope threatened to snap and for a moment

Ramsay   FUCKING PULL

Jack   The three men were holding on by what felt like just a few frayed strands

Ramsay   JACK

Jack   And I was above them, looking down into their faces bright and open with an electric panic and I felt how Strange it was to be looking at death suspended in mid-air

Ramsay   JACK FUCKING PULL

Jack   You Are real

Ramsay   PULL

Marlow   We send our men into the villages and we take the women and the children and we send out Their men to bring back rubber from the forest.

Edmund   Dearest Marlow, could you send some more money, please.

Marlow   We have brought guns and diseases with us, it is not difficult to take control.

Edmund   Dear Jack, would you mind sending a little money, please, I have nowhere to sleep and nothing to eat.

Marlow   If they do not bring enough back, we chop off the hands, the feet of their wives, their daughters, present the amputated hand or foot to the fathers and husbands and we send the men back out again.

Edmund   I am making my way towards London.

Marlow   It has proved a good incentive.

Edmund   Not mountains nor jungle, but London, Hello

Jack   We make it back down the mountain.

Edmund   hello

Jack   We eat. We drink.

Edmund   Um. hello I

Jack   We toast that we are alive, a celebration I have made many times now, though I feel no closer to understanding Why, why it is Me who gets not only to *live* but often at the

expense of others – Perhaps there is no reason, or perhaps
there is

Ramsay   Look this way

Jack   A camera

Ramsay   Hold still

Jack   May I

Ramsay   If you like.

Jack   How marvellous

Ramsay   Three years later, I scaled K2 and on the descent,
I died and just before I died, just as I was drifting In and
Out of consciousness, his voice arrived first, low and clear,
and then his face, and then his body, very real, very solid -

Jack   Don't go to sleep

Ramsay   he said

Jack   Don't fall asleep

Ramsay   he said

Jack   You have yet more

Ramsay   But I didn't. I didn't.

Marlow   They bring back more each day until there is no
more to bring back. We reunite many women and men, we
put families back together again. It is genuinely joyful to
witness.

Edmund   I hide myself in the luggage compartment of a
train until I am discovered and thrown off. I make much of
the journey on foot, I sleep in ditches and forests, outhouses
and parks, I drink by roadsides with men and I swear and I
dance and leer and I pretend to be an entirely different
person each night – perhaps that is how one Finds who one
really is – a series of attempts, of failures, of wearing an Idea
of what a person ought to be, of what a Man Looks like and

seeing if it fits, is that how you did it is that how You became
who You are were you just doing an impression of a Man

Charles   Your mouth is pink.

Edmund   .

Marlow   It is difficult

Charles   Do you paint it

Edmund   What

Charles   Your mouth, do you paint it

Edmund   no

Charles   Your eyelashes

Edmund   What

Charles   They are like spiders

Edmund   .

Marlow   It is difficult.

Charles   Do you curl them

Edmund   No

Charles   What colour is your tongue

Edmund   I

Charles   Show me

Edmund   I

Charles   Show me your tongue

Marlow   It was somehow difficult, to stand over them, with
all of their resources and many of their limbs, stacked up
behind us, but with them still Breathing, them still
containing Life and, and crucially, perhaps, the Memories,
more than the fucking Memories, the Physical fucking
Evidence of the *Trauma* do I mean *Trauma* yes I mean

fucking *Trauma* that is what I mean – *Trauma* of what They felt We had done to them.

Of what they felt

Jack   Hello

Edmund   Hello

Jack   Yes

Edmund   Hello

Jack   Edmund

Edmund   Sorry

.

It is Nice to say Hello to somebody and have it returned I have felt.

Not Here for.

.

Anyway.

Marlow   Of what They felt

Emilio   Not what we felt.

.

Marlow   What they felt

Emilio   Not what we felt you had done, what you Had done.

.

Rape. Starvation. Flagellation, Immolation. Dismemberment. Genocide.

Marlow   We left and

Emilio   Execution

Marlow   We Left and

Emilio   Massacre and torture

Marlow   Made our way back up the river

Emilio   The trees as they grow from root to sun have no value without us you know nothing without us

Marlow   Sloth and jaguar

Emilio   Before we saw your white sails upon our horizons we had a life

Marlow   Treefrog and macaw

Emilio   Defined by something other than trauma, you would feel something for us other than Pity

Marlow   Cotinga and tapir

Emilio   I had a wife and a father, a daughter and a son a son and a son and a daughter

Marlow   Caiman and iguana

Emilio   Each child born in the forest, each born at the base of a tree beneath the light of the moon or the heat of the sun, the cord cut by a palm reed and now mutilated or dead or fleeing because of You.

I was a fisherman my father was a fisherman my brother was a fisherman my sons were fishermen before before before before the before before the before, I used to tell my sons as we waded into the river away from the alligators and the catfish

Marlow   We find nickel.

Emilio   I used to tell my sons of the stories of the Amazon, the stories of the river, the stories of the people who have lived here before what you would recognise as the world began – God Tupã who married the goddess Arasy, the mother of the sky, whose home was the moon, the very same moon that hung above my sons as they entered the world, and Arasy and Tupã descended upon the Earth the morning after their wedding and together they created the rivers and the seas, the forests and the skies and that from clay and Yerba mate, blood from the short-tailed Nighthawk and leaves and a centipede, Man was made and Woman was made and all of HumanKind was made

Marlow   We find tin and we find copper.

Emilio   And a Warrior was born, a Warrior named Pirarucú was born and this warrior was brave, but arrogant, brave, but vain, brave but he liked to Anger the Gods and before all of the befores Tupã, the God of all Gods threw lightning bolts at him, threw lightning bolts at his heart and he was thrown into the river, this river, this river where we stand and he became the fish, he became the fish that we now catch, the Pirarucú fish, the fish my father caught and my grandfather caught and his grandfather caught and now we have no hands and now we have no afters and now the befores Torment us and now we have

Marlow   We find manganese and we find bauxite.

Emilio   And now we have nothing

Marlow   We find more rubber.

Emilio   And now we have nothing

Marlow   We find Gold.

Edmund   I am happy to see you, Jack.

Jack   .

Will you eat something

Edmund   Would you Like me to eat something

Jack   If you are hungry, Edmund, then you should eat.

.

There are clean clothes on the bed in your room

Edmund   You look so different and yet just the same

Jack   You should wash

Edmund   Ah.

Yes.

I was never very

.

I haven't been living in

I am sorry

Jack   What are your intentions, Edmund.

Edmund   I.

I do not know that I Have any – what should my intentions be – what are yours?

Jack   I have paid for these rooms for the next six months

Edmund   Oh

Jack   I will pay for longer if it suits you

Edmund   Will you stay

Jack   I will stay for tonight

Edmund   Oh.

Where will you go.

Jack   You have to Make Something of yourself now, Edmund

Edmund   Make Something

Of Myself

Jack   Yes

Edmund   I do not know that I have the pieces

Jack   Edmund

Edmund   Yes, sorry

Jack   The world is Available to you

Edmund   Is it

Jack   Of course it is

Edmund   I have not been able to see myself in it at all

Jack   Then you are not trying

Edmund   I'm sure you are right, I am sure of it

Jack   You have to Decide what you Want and then go out and Get it

Edmund   I

cannot fathom how to

Move through the world in that way I is that really how you live

Jack   You speak like a woman

Edmund   Do I?

Jack   You do

Edmund   I do, I am sorry – London looks exactly as I pictured it would look – Grey and Smog and Crowded with noise and buildings and people and hunger and greed and elbows and ambition and nothing of any surprise – do you hear from Marlow

Jack   I hear Of Marlow very frequently, but we are not in regular correspondence – slow down, you will choke

Edmund   Forgive me, I have not

Eaten in Company for

It is Terribly. Impressive, what he has Achieved

Jack   Yes, he is certainly Making his Fortunes you will call on the Bradshaws – an old associate of Father's, do you remember him

Edmund   no

Jack   He will help you find work

Edmund   Ah

Jack   You must be Willing

Edmund   yes

Jack   He has a daughter. Molly.

Perhaps you may make her your. Friend.

Edmund   .

Jack   It will Feel good, Edmund.

To make a friend.

Edmund   You have not made a friend

Jack   I have made plenty.

Edmund   Oh.

.

Will you be a mountaineer

Jack   No.

I have Done that

Edmund   The army

Jack   I have done that, I wish to find the Next thing to do

Edmund   Is that what one does? Constant Pursuit? Does that lead to contentment

Jack   I am not Seeking contentment Look Up

Edmund   Oh

Jack   Hold still

Edmund   What is that

Jack   A camera, look this way

Edmund   No, I

Jack   Here, boy

Edmund   Are you a photographer now

Jack   Constant Pursuit, Edmund, why can you not look up

Edmund   I am trying

Manolin   You have never been at sea

Jack   I have been on a boat

Manolin   As a passenger

Jack   Yes

Jack   Yes

Manolin   I have boys of thirteen on my ship

Jack   I Wanted More – I Wanted whatever the Opposite of Edmund was, I Wanted Horizon and Adventure and the Company of Men and Discovery and

Manolin   Why would I let you onboard when you have no experience

Jack   I do not know

Manolin   That is not a Good answer

Jack   No

Marlow   I build a glider and fly it two hundred and fifty yards

Jack   I have climbed mountains

Manolin   Congratulations

Marlow   I buy two newspapers and begin a third and then I buy two more

Jack   I have been to war

Manolin   Show me a man who hasn't

Marlow   I patent a two-cone roller bit which allows for drilling for petroleum in previously inaccessible places

Edmund   Constant Pursuit

Jack   I Want to come

Manolin   It will be Hard work

Jack   Good

Manolin   Many men have died on similar expeditions

Jack   Yes

Manolin   I don't need dead weight

Jack   Throw me overboard if I am no use.

Marlow   We drill for oil and we drill for gas and I found the Marlow Roman Aircraft Company and am on a quest to the middle of the Earth and beyond our atmosphere and I make more money than any man has ever made and I buy a Spring from a man in France

Bernard (*in French*)   It makes no money

Marlow   And I bottle the water

Bernard (*in French*)   I've lost everything to it

Marlow   And I sell it to the English as the Champagne of Water and make a small fortune

Jack   I have not the sea legs I had hoped for.

Edmund   Dearest Jack, I have called upon the Bradshaws as you asked and they were very kind, as you said, and his daughter, Molly, is very pretty, as you said and all will be well, as you said.

Jack   I fear I barely have any legs at all, I vomit and I collapse and I press my cheeks against the solid wooden floor of the ship's cabin and when we get there, when we get to the ice I am Overwhelmed – it stretches itself out like a body on a slab – the sky gapes above and you find yourself, I find myself, looking for its edges, searching for its Teeth, but there is nothing, no line between land and sky, between God and Man between the Stars and my Boots.

Edmund   He has found me some employment as an assistant projectionist at a cinema and Molly gave me some books and some paper and has said that she will Show me London and they gave me Dinner and told me stories and Molly played the piano and truthfully, Jack, kindness is more dangerous than I had thought it to be. Kindness is what I thought I was seeking but when they said goodnight and pressed my hands in theirs and squeezed my cheek and closed the door I felt myself Full of a white hot rage that they were not taking me in as their own, that they did not love me as I long to be loved as I have never been loved but no matter no matter

Jack   On the ice I saw Uncle John.

Marlow   Someone suggests that I should step into Politics

Prufrock   You ought to go into Politics

Jack   I saw Uncle John and I saw Edmund.

Marlow   Many people suggest that I ought to Step Into Politics

Prufrock   You really ought to step into politics

Jack   They stood at opposite ends of a tundra – John covered in blood, a gun in his hands, beckoning, and Edmund on the floor in a dress, half of his face missing and reaching towards me and when I went to photograph them they both disappeared

Edmund   Dear Edmund, there is a Man who comes to the cinema most days and after each film he says

Leo   Did you enjoy it

Edmund   And he brings me books

Leo   Milton

Edmund   And he asks me what I Think

Leo   'Better to reign in Hell, than Serve in Heaven'

Edmund   Yes

Leo   You understand?

Edmund   He does not laugh at my responses or recoil at my silence, we swim in the Lido the ponds and we drink in pubs

Leo   I am married to a woman I detest

Edmund   We walk on the Heath and we cycle through the rose garden at Regent's Park and he takes me to the zoo and we watch the Wolves and

Leo   I am married to a woman who makes my Skin Crawl

Edmund   He is a Professor at a university

Leo   All Women Make My Skin Crawl

Edmund   Perhaps I have made a Friend

Leo   Their Faces and their Legs and their Holes and their Stupidity and their incessant Wanting of things made of Fabric or Glass or Porcelain or China

Edmund   But sometimes he Says things that make my hands Tremble and my heart feel light and not in a way that Excites me but something Closer to Fear

Leo   You look frightened

Edmund   I am sorry

Leo   That is how you respond to almost anything I say

Edmund   I am sorry

Leo   Everything used to frighten Me too it is impossible to not be disappointed but his

Mouth

Edmund   Perhaps I should go home

Leo   Your eyes are so Big

Edmund   I

Leo   Open your Mouth

Edmund   I

Leo   I want to see inside it

Edmund   I should go home

Leo   Do you want me to Kiss you

Edmund   No

Leo   You do

Edmund   I am sorry

Leo   I can hear your Heart

Edmund   No, sir

Leo   I should kiss you out of pity

Edmund   no

Leo   You are so full of Need

Edmund   I am

Leo   Of Want

Edmund   I Am but Not

Leo   It's going like a machine gun and his face is damp and pale and covered in sweat and

I clamp him against a wall his body like a question mark and I kiss him out of pity

He kisses him.

Edmund   No

Leo   In an alleyway

Edmund   no

Leo   Out of pity

Edmund   no

Leo   Until he folds into a ball on the pavement and I return home to my papers and my wife

Jack   On the journey home my fever worsens and the boat seems to be only occupied by ghosts

Marlow   Put your thoughts in the mouth of a politician and nobody will listen, put them in print beneath a striking headline and alongside a salacious story of a murder and it will somehow seep in

Clifford   You ought to be in prison

Jack   When we get back to England I return to my Father's house and through my fever and beneath Marlow's newspapers and bottled water and Edmund's letters I find myself beginning to write

Edmund   I have not left my rooms in weeks

Marlow   This country is in decline, has lost its militant values, has become soft in its pursuit of pacifism and nationalisation, wants to give everybody exactly the same and no longer reward the brilliant and the rich, the well-educated and the brave – I fly planes and beat records I have already set I buy film studios and own actresses and build a casino in a city called Las Vegas and

Clifford   You're responsible for a genocide

Marlow   I buy a telescope and make improvements and somebody travels above the Kármán line and I branch out into space exploration

Clifford   You are responsible for a genocide

Marlow   I build hospitals and fund medical research and have galleries named after me

Clifford   You are Responsible for a Fucking Genocide – I write letters I write reports I write papers but he owns everything he buys everything he owns everyone he buys everyone I was a doctor and a missionary and I lose my wife and my family in my obsession to bring Marlow Roman to justice for the crimes that he committed and I write papers and letters and reports and then one day instead I fire a gun at him as he is leaving a hotel

Edmund   guns guns guns guns guns

Clifford   and I miss and I hit someone else and I languish in jail and I attempt a hunger strike in the hope That might gain me some attention but it does not and instead I die

Edmund   men die

Clifford   And the day after my death he is watching a cricket match and his newspapers all fail to report on my death and it is as though I was never here at all

Edmund   I have not left my rooms in months

Jack   I sit in the garden where my dogs slept I sit in the library where my brother played I sit at the table where my Father died I lie in the bedroom where my Mother died and my brother was born and I scale more of the world than any man has as I write

Edmund   I lie flat on the floor or I curl up in a ball I imagine I am a fox as someone knocks

Officer   Mr Roman

Edmund   No, hammers

Officer   Mr Roman

Edmund   Upon my door

Officer   Mr Roman, can you open the door please, this is the police

Jack   Nobody wants the book

Officer Mr Roman

Jack And so I write another

Officer Mr Roman

Marlow I Am Bored

Officer Hello

Edmund Hello

Edmund Can I help you

Officer Do you mind if I ask you some questions.

Edmund Um.

No.

Jack And so I write another.

Officer How long have you lived here, Mr Roman.

Edmund Um.

Eight months or so?

Officer And what do you do for work?

Edmund Nothing. Currently.

Officer How do you pay for your rooms.

Edmund My brothers send me money.

Officer That is very kind of them.

Edmund Yes.

They are kind.

.

Officer Are you friendly with your neighbours.

Edmund .

I can't say that I am.

It is Not that I am Unfriendly

Officer   No

Edmund   But I keep myself to myself as it were.

Officer   Yes

.

Edmund   Is that alright.

Officer   That's a strange question

Edmund   Is it? I'm sorry.

Officer   Half of your neighbours don't know of your existence

Edmund   Ah

Officer   Quite a job that, given you share a bathroom with six other families

Edmund   I try not to be a nuisance

Officer   If only more people had that attitude, Mr Roman, are you familiar with the gentleman who lives on the floor beneath you – Mr Wilson?

Edmund   No, sir

Officer   Or Mr Percival, across the hall

Edmund   No, sir

Officer   Did you ever make the acquaintance of a Mr Neville – a homeless man who frequents the local pubs

Edmund   I do not leave my rooms, sir

Officer   Are you a Homosexual, Mr Roman.

Edmund   .

I.

I hardly know what I. Or who I. I am barely Here I think but.

.

I am nothing.

Officer   .

May I ask where you were on the evening of the 7th of March.

Edmund   I.

Would have been here, officer.

.

Officer   Did you Hear anything Unusual that evening.

Edmund   .

No, sir.

Officer   See anything that seemed in any way. Suspicious.

Edmund   No, sir.

Officer   May I ask where you were on the evening of the 8th of March

Edmund   Here, sir

Officer   And on the 9th of March

Edmund   Here, sir

Officer   You are here a great deal

Edmund   I am, sir

Officer   And may anyone Vouch for that

Edmund   Vouch

Officer   Vouch

Edmund   Vouch

Officer   Is there anyone who could corroborate your Testimony that you were Here

Edmund   I am all alone, sir, I am sorry, sir

.

May I ask why you're asking me

Officer   Those three men have been murdered.

Edmund   .

Oh.

Officer   Oh.

Edmund   My mouth is dry.

Officer   They were three particularly vicious attacks

Edmund   Oh

Officer   Oh

Edmund   Oh

Officer   I find it impossible that you did not hear anything

Edmund   It's a very noisy

place it is not Unusual to hear people Screaming I have become accustomed to

blocking it out may I open a window

Officer   It is your home

Edmund   some Air

Jack   Hello

Edmund   Hello

Jack   yes

Edmund   Thank you for coming

Jack   This is becoming a habit

Edmund   You have grown taller

Jack   You have shrunk

Edmund   I am sorry

Jack   For what

Edmund   For all the trouble I have caused you

Jack   And yourself

Edmund   I have no self – you are a writer now

Jack   I wrote a book and nobody wanted it

Edmund   I found it most interesting

Jack   Nobody else did

Edmund   You are brave to write the truth

Jack   Am I

Edmund   Father always spoke of the importance of the written word, I believe he would be proud

Jack   I do not think that I want that man's Pride hold still

Edmund   Marlow arranged for a lawyer

Jack   Yes

Edmund   The lawyer wants me to lie

Jack   You should do as he says

Edmund   I do not want to lie

Jack   For your liberty

Edmund   I am so very sorry

Jack   Hold still

Edmund   Jack, I did not do it

Jack   Marlow's lawyer will get you off, Marlow's lawyers seem terribly accomplished at Getting People Off things that they Explicitly Did Do

Edmund   I Didn't do it

Jack   Look down

Edmund   I need You to know that I did not do it, that matters more to me than anything else I

Jack   Look this way

Edmund   I love you

Jack   Hold still

Edmund   Have I said the wrong thing

Jack   Father was a cruel man

Edmund   no

Jack   I saw what he did to you

Edmund   I did not do it Jack, you must believe me

Jack   I saw what he Made you

Edmund   You do believe me, don't you.

Jack.

.

Clarissa   Well you've made a lot of people Terribly angry, haven't you?

Jack   She had the most extraordinary eyes I had ever seen. Large and unblinking, kind yet serious. I couldn't move. Pinned to the spot. I was staring.

Clarissa   You are a cause célèbre, is that terribly fun?

Jack   Since the publication of my latest book I found myself being invited to parties and dinners and galas and exhibitions and readings and theatrical openings as a fashionable sort of accessory to any event – the hostess of any one of these seemed to enjoy the little gasp or open mouths that my arrival usually inspired.

Clarissa   Your own brother, how very exciting

Jack   The book I had written had caused a sensation – the photographs I had taken of my brother in his grey prison uniform, his head bowed, his eyes wet and wild, and the text that accompanied – streams of consciousness, court transcripts, interviews with Edmund and my own fictionalised accounts of the lives of the murdered men, and that of my brother – all of this marked a New Form and people were both as thrilled and appalled by That notion as the fact that I seemed to Flirt with both his Guilt and

his Innocence with a lightness that did not correspond to the Brutality of the three murders of which he was accused.

Edmund   In books, people say I love you and they often have it returned

Marlow   You have been found Not Guilty

Edmund   Yes

Marlow   Stand up

Edmund   Yes

Marlow   Straight

Edmund   Yes

Marlow   You have been given an opportunity

Edmund   Yes

Marlow   To begin again

Edmund   In books and in cinema, people reach out their arms and someone steps into them – dear Jack, congratulations on your book I could not read past the first line I wish that the night father died he had turned the gun on me instead it is hopeless

Marlow   I have bought you a house

Edmund   Please don't

Marlow   I will take it off you if you continue to be such a fucking disappointment

Edmund   Please don't give it to me in the first place

Marlow   So that you may Make something of yourself

Edmund   I have not the pieces

Marlow   Stand up straight

Edmund   I cannot

Marlow   Lift your chin

Edmund   no

Marlow   Try harder

Edmund   I want to crawl.

Marlow   Don't be so fucking pathetic

Edmund   I am truly sorry to be such a disappointment, I think, perhaps, that you want me to be something I am not Able to be – I think, actually, no, perhaps, that everybody wants me to Be Something and I am just not Able to Be

Marlow   You're just not Trying hard enough

Edmund   I feel I have tried

Marlow   Life is supposed to be hard

Edmund   Is it supposed to be impossible?

Marlow   It. It. It can. Feel Hard but

Edmund   Marlow, what was our Mother like.

Marlow   She.

Jack   Amongst these nonstop events I found that I was Bored by the

Marlow   She
.

cocktails and the pale champagne and   She

the pink salmon and the string section   .

of the orchestra or the spiked heels or   She

the exposed collarbone or the elbow   .

length gloves or the red roses in   She

tuxedo lapels or *I loved your book I*   .

loved your book I just Loved your book   .

in rooms where even the highest   .

ceilings felt I was being Compressed but   .

Clarissa Castorp – daughter of a Swedish   .

banker and perhaps the most eligible   .

deb in London – was different.   .

Marlow   She was Kind, Edmund.

Edmund   Give me something else.

Marlow   I have nothing else – you killed her and I barely knew her but she Was kind, Edmund, she was. Soft.

.

Edmund   Do you think she would have

not been Proud of me, I cannot offer anything to.

But.

Might she have Liked me?

Marlow   .

Clarissa   Do you speak with your Mouth or only communicate via the written word

Jack   Did you read it

Clarissa   He speaks

Jack   Did you

Clarissa   Oh no I'm just here for the drinks.

Yes I read it, of course I read it, everyone has read it.

Jack   And?

Clarissa   And?

Jack   Well, what did you think?

Clarissa   You are like a little boy with your hands held out in front of you begging for your sweets or your Mother's praise

.

I thought it was

Not boring.

Jack   Not boring?

Clarissa   I didn't like your central character.

He was Weak.

He didn't stand for anything.

People rarely stand for anything in reality but they certainly Ought to in literature otherwise what is the point.

.

Marlow   Are you alright

Rosa   I   **Clarissa**   I write.

Marlow   Here, take my hand

Rosa   Everybody is looking

Marlow   Just look at me

Jack   What was that

Rosa   I   **Clarissa**   *I* write

Marlow   Are you in pain

Rosa   Yes

Marlow   Where

Rosa   This isn't how it happened – My ankle

Marlow   I will find you somewhere private to sit

Rosa   Everybody is looking

Jack   What do you write

Marlow   Just look at me

Rosa   I'm trying   **Clarissa**   I

Marlow   Who is that man

Clarissa   I try to write about

Marlow   Do you know him

Rosa   It's fine

Marlow   It isn't fine, that isn't what Love is

Rosa (*to the audience*)   Can we stop, can we make it very
Clear that This isn't how this happened.

It didn't happen this way. None of it happened this way.

Marlow   Men aren't allowed to Treat women like that

Rosa   It's fine I am fine

Marlow   You are trembling

Rosa   I am cold, that is all

Marlow   He has hurt you

Rosa   this isn't how it happened

Marlow   I will talk to him

Rosa   please don't

Marlow   I will have one of my associates talk to him

Rosa   Please don't

Edmund   I didn't do it.

Rosa   What is your name?

Marlow   What is yours.

Jack   Would you like to dance.

Clarissa   Nobody else is dancing.

Jack   I don't care. I want to hold you in my arms.

Clarissa   Oh.

Rosa   My name is Rosa.

Marlow   Marlow. My name is Marlow Roman.

.

The women in this section maybe speak into microphones at the front of the stage – or at least somewhere that feels new / not with the men.

Edmund   Dearest Jack, Congratulations on your recent engagement. I saw the announcement in the papers.

Clarissa (*almost whispered, an urgency*)   I write. I have always written. It is the only thing I ever wanted to do. My father said do not marry that man, do not marry that man, he will squash you even if he doesn't mean to which he will not, you will be typing His stories and his work will always mean more than yours ever could but that was how things Used to be we agreed we would write and travel and live in Italy and eat good food and Write and

Edmund   Dearest Marlow, Congratulations on your marriage, I hope that you and Rosa will be very happy together.

Rosa (*almost whispered, an urgency*)   It was essentially Kidnap which wasn't to say I didn't Like him wasn't to say there was no Attraction there because there Was, there was something altogether primal and uncomfortable and violent and exciting but it didn't happen This way, he didn't actually Speak to me that evening – I was engaged to another man, a kind man, a man who I had known since we were children, a man who had made a reasonable amount of money and who Loved me, I think, and who I, I suppose I loved, I suppose if, at the time, someone had asked me – do you love this man who you have known since you were a child I would have said, confidently, happily, yes, I love him very much – and our whole lives were mapped out, we would have married and had children and lived in a nice house where I would have died – but Marlow, Marlow Decided that my life was to be different, Marlow Decided that I was to be his and I do not know what love is anymore, but I could tell you what Excitement is I could tell you what it is to be turned into an Object and then be Claimed by a Man with more wealth than I knew was possible and I could tell you that all I thought I was as a person disappeared because he Wanted Me and I wanted to be wanted and wanted and That evening, my fiancé, that Kind and Quite Forgettable man – what did he look like actually, I could not tell you, I think he had eyebrows – That evening, he got a little drunk, and a little possessive and he didn't like the Cut of my dress and he had Gripped me by the wrist and Marlow crossed the room in one quick move and Grabbed him by the Throat and Threw him against the wall and Hit him again and again and again and again blood spraying and everyone Screaming and then he Turns to me, covered in this other man's blood and he just Stares at me for a full minute, his breath heavy, this other man On the floor and his expression Wild and Frightening and Interesting and Abhorrent and the Next day he came to my home and he told me in his own language that my city was a ShitHole and that I wouldn't be Safe here and that he wanted to take me back to London with him as his wife and I Realised as I watched his fists clench and unclench as he spoke that he would kill me or protect me or both but not neither and that I would never fully close my eyes ever again.

Edmund   Dear Jack, congratulations on the safe arrival of your daughter, I wonder if I will ever meet her. I imagine not, but I have an image of her in my mind and I will grow her there and visit her daily and she and I are meeting on another, imagined plane.

Clarissa (*almost whispered, an urgency*)   A baby. there's a baby.

I am turned into a soft shapeless pulp and there is a baby here now she will always be here now and he stretches the days by not coming home until it is dark and my body is like a little doll poked with needles and I can't hold my arms up and open windows and light fittings are shaped like answers to a problem I never wanted in the first fucking place and

Edmund   Dear Marlow, another boy! And you named him after Father. How wonderful. I do marvel at how Successful you and Jack are, it seems quite extraordinary to me, too bright to look at somehow, too much sun, too much heat, I almost can't bear it. The newspapers write constantly of how much Money you have made, how much Political influence you have, what an Innovator you are and I think back to when we were children and Search for some origin of it but. We did not have much time together so.

Rosa (*almost whispered, an urgency*)   We have four children in as many years – twins and then one two more and each time they have Just left my body he announces his face red with pride as though he has just done an enormous shit that he is exceedingly proud of – that he wants another but I like motherhood I like the shape of my belly with a baby in there I like being full of milk I like my body having this other Purpose I like the fluids and the mess and I like their little round cheeks and their rolls of fat around their wrists and the dimples where their knuckles should be I even like it when they scream because really they are screaming for me they are absolutely full of a furious and devoted Need for me and that is very compelling and we live in a Big house and Marlow just cannot stop making money it Pours out of every bit of him so I have dresses and curtains and beautiful furniture and a view of the park and a cook and a maid and a nanny and another nanny and another maid and private dance lessons and private piano lessons to take on my very own grand piano in my very own ballroom and a French tutor who comes on a Wednesday and who I fuck in one of the million bedrooms whilst my husband is somewhere else making more money to buy me more things

Edmund   Dear Jack, congratulations on your latest book, the papers describe it as Daring and Original and name You as the Voice of Our Times and this morning I foraged for blackberries whilst planes flew overhead towards London. I suppose you and Marlow must be fighting again. I pray for you both, and for your families and wonder if you ever read these letters and wonder sometimes why it is you never wrote more than a word or two back, though I do not blame you, I just wonder.

Clarissa (*almost whispered, an urgency*)   Another baby drops in and then out of me and someone has the audacity to suggest that I might be losing my fucking mind I hear whispers constantly and planes fly overhead and Men go to war again and I wipe mouths and stir porridge and hang nappies and fall asleep in chairs with babies on my lap and my father says I told you so and I consider pretending to go mad just so that somebody else might hold a baby my arms ache and Men return from war and Men go to war and Men return from war and cannot speak anymore I run the bath too hot and I leave the baby in the garden for a whole night and I walk through a sheet of glass and he finds me with a rope in my hand and I can't stop laughing and I can't stop shaking and then I suppose I am no longer pretending I suppose I might actually have had the audacity to go fucking mad and he sends me to a Beautiful building in the mountains called a Sanatorium and I don't have to hold a baby I can just lie on a bed in a room with yellow wallpaper and look at the crocuses on the lawn outside my window and I can swim in the freezing cold pool and I can go to sleep if I want to if I am able to I can go to sleep whilst my husband travels around Europe fucking everything that Moves and then returning to his Father's house where I hear he has taken several lovers and is now a passionate advocate for Yoga and he is writing he is writing and writing and writing he is writing books and essays and poems and articles and some of those stories seem to be the story of my fucking life but at this moment at This moment I am too tired or too full of delicious fucking pills to actually care and sometimes they put electrodes on my head and send an electrical current through my brain and sometimes I go for walks and take the Air and sometimes I talk to a Man for hours about what he believes is the envy I possess for my husband's penis and I can look at a blank sheet of paper and imagine what

I

What I

What I

might write again now that I am all alone.

Marlow (*to* **Jack**)   Hello.

Jack (*to* **Marlow**)   Hello.

They look to **Edmund**. *They do not say hello. He does not say anything back. A beat.*

Edmund   Dear Jack, I was sorry to read about your wife's illness. The papers seemed to be salacious in their reporting I have found of late that I cannot be in rooms anymore ceilings threaten to collapse upon me, walls flatten me, they are Airless one cannot breathe or move or Think within them the Centre cannot hold and so I have become adept at life on the road, which will make it hard for you to contact me and I have decided that I shall no longer contact you or Marlow or anybody else ever again and I feel quite free because of it. If I cease to exist for anybody else am I really here.

I never imagined I would lead a life this lonely, and some part of me Longs for company as I did so desperately when I was a child – specifically yours and Marlow's, that of my kin, my family. I do not say that hoping to be taken in, I am happy and proud that you have both found love and homes and are building families and truthfully, I don't believe I know how to be among people in this world without ruining everything.

I make fire and I skin squirrels and forage for sorrel and I sleep amongst clumps of bluebells underneath the nests of wrens and at night I make myself very small and say a prayer for Father and a prayer for Mother and a prayer for Marlow and a prayer for you, Jack, but never a prayer for myself for I now have no self and perhaps I never did.

The sound of planes overhead, gunfire and bombs grows to a deafening pitch.

Part Three

SUMMER

We're in the garden and kitchen of the Roman family home. It's been turned a sort of commune. Bucolic. Birdsong. Soft, warm light. Greenery and flowers and just a general sort of feeling of abundance. There are two cameras set up. Maybe there's music playing from a record player. It feels like animals live here – chickens and dogs, pigs and horses. On the lawn in front of the house is a big dining table and a barbecue. To the left of the lawn is a very homemade sauna, and next to it an outdoor shower. We can see inside through a glass door or window – **Benny** *is sitting in it.*

After a moment, **Jack** *enters, followed by* **Esther**. *She holds a camera in one hand – she's filming him – and a book in the other. He is in a swimming costume. As they speak he leaves the room to fetch a towel, dries himself, leaves to fetch clothes, gets undressed and changed into clothes whilst they talk. He lights a cigarette once he is dressed. Maybe she puts the camera down or sets it up on a tripod. This conversation is light – or at least it begins in a way that feels light.*

Esther   'Probably some of this is true but why would anyone give a fuck about the truth anyway, why don't you get on with living.'

Jack   .

Uh huh

Esther   Feels like a different tone for you

Jack   Does it

Esther   Mmhmm

Jack   In what way

Esther   Uh

It's a pretty aggressive opener

Jack   Aggressive?

Esther   I mean. Yeah, I think so?

Jack   You don't like it

Esther   I don't know yet

Jack   How come

Esther   I mean Just

I suppose there's a Gut reaction and then there's the more Thoughtful one that follows – hopefully

Jack   Is that always how it works / for you

Esther   / I don't know I just mean.

Is it helpful to use words like – Like and DisLike when you're talking about Art, it doesn't matter

Jack   I think it matters

Esther   Yeah

Jack   Are you asking me a question

Esther   No?

Jack   There's this upward inflection

Esther   Oh

Jack   You should swim it feels Incredible

Esther   You swim every day

Jack   I do

Esther   How come

Jack   Because I Like It

And I do tend to be engaged with Like and Dislike in all aspects of my life – art, food, music, fucking, drugs

Esther   Okay

Jack   I'm sorry if that's disappointing

Esther   No

Jack   Don't you think an opening sentence should be Arresting?

Should grab its Reader

Esther   I guess

Jack   How will this film begin

Esther   I don't know yet

Jack   Really

Esther   No.

.

Is that bad?

Jack   I don't know, is it?

.

Anna *enters from the house and starts preparing some food. A salad. Washing some potatoes.*

Hi

Anna   Uh huh

Jack   Is this what you wanted, Esther?

Are you getting what you need?

Esther   Uh

Jack   Are you asking all the questions you wanted to ask

Esther   Are there questions You think I should be asking

Jack   What should Esther be asking us

Anna   Huh

Jack   What are you making

Anna   Salad

Jack   Who's doing the meat

Anna   Timothy's getting it

Jack   D'you want to help, Esther

Esther   Um

Sure

Jack   You don't have to

Esther   No, it's fine, that sounds

Jack   Could she help you, Anna

Anna   If you like

Esther   Okay

Anna   No, if You like

Jack   I like

Esther   He's in charge?

Anna   We wouldn't use those words

Jack   Or peel some potatoes

Esther   Okay

Jack   Everything's from the garden

Esther   Uh huh

They start to make a meal together. The women focus on preparing a salad, on vegetables. **Jack** *sits at a table and drinks a beer.*

Esther   Is that one of the things that um, is that maybe, Values or

Jack   Values

Esther   Yeah, like, what are the Values of your Community?

Jack   Community is a good word. Family.

I don't know, Anna, what do you think?

Anna   We're a family.

Esther   A family who grow vegetables and ride horses and do yoga together?

Jack   That sounds like a nice family

Esther   Uh huh.

Is that the

Extent of it?

Jack   I think it would be very difficult to

Summarise our lives for you in one sentence.

Esther   Uh huh.

What does your

Other family think about you living here

Anna   I don't have another family

Esther   Your Birth family, the people you Grew up with or

Anna   They don't exist

Esther   Something happened to them

Anna   They never were so there was nothing that could happen To them

Esther   But.

Where were you Before you came here?

Anna   I wasn't.

Jack   Esther doesn't like my new book

Anna   Esther's a fucking pig then

Esther   I

I didn't

I didn't Say that I

It's a Different direction perhaps I What do You think about it

Anna   I don't think, we're not here to think, cut the tomatoes

Esther   Okay

What do you mean you're not here to think

Anna   Jack thinks for us, we get to be empty.

.

Esther *looks at* **Jack**. *He smiles, sort of shrugs – who knows.*

Esther   What do You think about that then?

Jack   About what.

Esther   About what Anna just said

Jack   You want to get inside everybody's head and dig around

Anna   Fucking government

Esther   No, it's just.

What Anna said is. Quite Extreme

Jack   Is it?

.

Esther   She just – sorry – Anna just said that she's Empty

Jack   She said she Gets to be Empty.

Esther   Okay

Jack   You have a problem with that

Esther   I don't have a Problem with it, I'm just.

It's.

Extreme

Jack   Extreme?

Anna   It sounds like you have a problem with that

Jack   I think we just have to Allow people to be In whatever they are currently feeling and who are we to speak to whatever it is that Anna is Feeling.

.

Esther   Can you tell me about the comet.

Anna   No one needs to be Told about the comet, you just have to open your eyes.

Esther   Sure, I just.

I feel like I Have opened my eyes

Anna   You haven't

Esther   And I haven't seen it

Anna   Yeah, then you haven't opened your eyes

Esther   Well, can you tell me about it then

Anna   Why should we Explain something to you if you can't be bothered to just Look Up.

.

Esther   I mean.

I have – I *have* looked up, and I have Spoken to some Scientists

Anna   Oh she's Spoken to some Scientists

Esther   You don't like scientists

Anna   I don't trust people who are so Certain about shit that we Can't be certain about

Esther   But You're certain

Anna   Because I can fucking See it *With* my own eyes.

Esther (*still light*)   Yeah, I mean I.

I suppose I don't know what else I can do to impress upon you how much I have tried to engage with your Theory

Anna   It's not a Theory

Esther   I'd love to hear about it in your words

Anna   The End Is Coming.

.

Esther   Okay.

Okay and.

Do you know When or

Anna   Try harder.

.

Esther   This is something You believe?

Jack   I think

When you use language like Believe

or Theory it feels

And I know this won't be your intention, but it feels

Antagonistic

Anna   Exactly

Jack   Patronising

Anna   *Yes*

Esther   That's not my intention.

Jack   The only useful thing I feel I can say to you, on the matter of the comet is.

Keep looking.

Keep looking up.

Be open.

.

Esther   Okay.

Thank you.

Anna   fuck you

Esther   Excuse me

Jack   Anna.

.

Esther   Can you

Speak a little about how it all started I.

Jack   How what started.

Esther   You were living in London

Jack   I was

Esther   You

Fought

in the War

Anna   *The* war

Jack   Unfortunately, I fought in several

Esther   Your wife

Jack (*still light*)   I think I'm interested in Now, in Here. In how to be very Present in a moment

Esther   Okay.

.

Your wife, though, Clarissa, she was committed to a sanatorium.

Jack   Do you eat meat?

Esther   .

I do.

Jack   .

Clarissa has spent some time in a sanatorium, yes.

Esther   She was a writer also.

Jack   She certainly Wanted to write.

Esther   She

if I can. contradict.

.

I mean.

She Has written

Jack   Yes, she Has written since, but you said Was, when we met she had not yet written.

Esther   You

.

Jack   Yes?

Esther   Wrote About her

Jack   She featured

Esther   She says you

Wrote her life, you Stole her story

Committed her to print, to a sanatorium where she was –

(*Reading her notes.*) 'Stuffed with pills, held down in bathtubs, strapped to beds with leather restraints whilst they fired electrodes into my exhausted but once brilliant brain, all on the instruction of my husband, my concerned husband, my terribly worried husband who was nowhere to be seen, writing novels about me in the Rivera and fucking anything that moved.'

Jack   Is that a question?

Esther   I suppose I am asking whether you agree with that statement.

Jack   Statement?

Sorry, which part was a Statement

Esther   Uh well I mean – maybe Statement isn't the right

Jack   Uh huh

Timothy *enters, holding a brace of rabbits. He puts them down on the side, washes his hands, gets a beer.* **Anna** *begins to skin and gut the rabbits.*

Anna   If it's not the right word then maybe you shouldn't say it

Esther   I

Anna   If you're not Sure of what you're saying, maybe you shouldn't speak

Esther   Is that why you let Jack speak For you

Anna   I don't Let him, it's not Letting, it just Is – fucking Scientists

Esther   I

Jack   Look, in terms of Clarissa – who, I feel for very much – I'm very conscious of how Difficult it was for her, for Women generally, but – I don't know that it is a – let's use your word – a Statement – I can agree or disagree with – I wrote something and she feels a certain way about what I wrote, I can't see that there is anything else to say.

It was, perhaps, exacerbated by the fact that my work has been, at times, read very widely and impacted the culture and her

Work

if we can call it that.

Has not.

Esther   .

Jack   What.

Esther   Well.

I agree that Clarissa's work hasn't necessarily

Permeated

Jack   Good word

Esther   The culture in the same way that yours has

Jack   No.

Esther   .

But.

Jack   But.

Esther   .

Her work has

perhaps

Jack   You're very tentative

Esther   Offered a Reframing

Jack   Ah

Esther   Of yours.

.

There wasn't a question there I

Jack   No.

Esther   Sorry

Jack   .

Esther   Do you read your reviews?

Jack   No.

Not anymore.

Esther   Since they became more critical?

Jack   Are you Aware of how antagonistic you're coming across

Esther   I think I'm just asking questions

Anna   Something's rotten at the middle of you

Esther   .

Okay?

Jack   No. I don't mind the criticism. I'm interested in the dialogue.

Esther   But

Jack   They have begun to write about what they Want it to be rather than what it Is and that is Vandalism

Esther   Vandalism

Jack   To an artistic process, yes

Esther   'Jack Roman, once the greatest writer of his generation, has become a parody of himself, bloated and self-obsessed, lazy and derisive toward his reader at every turn'

Jack   Do you agree with it

Esther   I don't know yet

Jack   What reaction are you hoping to provoke by Sharing that with me

Esther   I don't have an Intention, I want your honest response

Jack   Being misinterpreted is Hurtful

Esther   Yes

Jack   Stop doing it then.

Esther   .

Anna   Submit.

It feels So Good.

To Submit.

.

Esther   You don't see your children.

Jack   I see my children, my children don't see me.

Esther   Is That a joke?

Jack   I don't think so.

.

Esther   This is the house you grew up in.

Jack   This was my childhood home, yes.

This was my father's house. Or. At least the man I Thought was my father.

He shot himself in this kitchen, in that corner – I haven't painted over it. There's still some blood spatter if you're interested.

I bought it a little after my wife was – what was the word you used? Committed. You eat rabbit?

Esther   I

I've never had it before but I'll try it

Jack   Good girl

Esther   Why did you buy it?

Jack   The house?

Esther   Uh huh.

Jack   I wanted it.

Esther   .

Why?

Jack *smiles. Shrugs.*

Esther   Why would you want to be in the place where something so Awful happened

Timothy   Who says it's awful? Death isn't Awful.

Esther   Well.

Timothy   It's a part of life.

Esther   Yes but.

A man shooting himself in the head in front of his two sons Is fairly unequivocally awful.

Timothy   Why.

He Wanted to do something and he Followed through. I think that's quite beautiful.

Esther   .

He Shot himself

Timothy   Yeah you keep focusing on that – is it the Mess that's the problem?

Esther   It's the proximity to his Young children

Timothy   He could've done it upstairs with a pill – but then there's vomit, or taken himself off to a hotel and put a note on the door – a warning – do not enter, leave this room unexamined for a thousand years – until we can be certain that I have turned into dust – he could've disappeared, or taken himself off to War – there's Always a war to go and die in – Death has to be Witnessed, it has to be Acknowledged and Looked at, it is a Part of us and now Henry is a part of us – what he Did for his sons that day is an extraordinary thing, a gift. He Showed them that Life and Death. There's a whisper between them.

Jack   Thank you, Timothy

Timothy   It's all you.

.

Esther   I disagree.

Timothy   That is your right, but maybe you'd be more comfortable disagreeing with us at a distance.

Esther   .

Why are you here?

Timothy   Why are You?

Esther   I'm making a film.

Timothy   Go deeper.

Esther   .

Can I ask.

Where are you From

Timothy   .

No.

I don't think you Can ask that

Esther   Why not

Timothy   .

Esther   You were born in South America

Anna   Why are you asking questions that you know the answer to fucking police

Esther   Your Father

Timothy   What about him?

Esther   .

Is there anything you'd like to say about him?

Timothy   What do You want to say about him

Esther   Well he.

He's quite famous

Timothy   Was he

Esther   Yeah, I think your father is pretty well known

Timothy   Okay

Esther   He was an activist

Timothy   I don't think about him

Esther   Your Mother and sisters had their hands and feet chopped off

Timothy   Yes

Esther   You Fled

Timothy   I don't think of it that way – I came Here, it wasn't about Fleeing somewhere, Leaving there, but being drawn to Here – Here was where I was supposed to be

Esther   How did your father feel about you being here

Timothy   If I have a father it's Jack

Esther   You've made a white man your father, your God

Anna   Fucking hell

Timothy   You think I'm enslaved and you're free

Esther   Honestly? A bit

Anna   BURN THE WITCH

Jack   Anna

Esther   No?

Timothy   I don't think about it that way.

Esther   Why

Timothy   Are you in pain?

Esther   Excuse me

Timothy   You seem like a person In Pain

Esther   Okay

Timothy   I used to be in pain

Esther   Okay

Timothy   Before we were here, we were all in such pain, Esther

Esther   Okay

Timothy   Do you know what it feels like to have all of your pain Wiped away.

Thank you, Jack

Anna   Thank you, Jack

Jack   I love you both, very much. I'm very proud of you.

.

Esther (*to* **Jack**)   Do you see your brothers?

Jack   No. Do you?

Esther   .

They have taken very different paths.

.

Jack   Did you want me to respond.

Esther   Ideally.

Jack   They have.

Different from me, different from one another.

Esther   Marlow is one of the richest men in the world.

Jack   I hear that.

Esther   And Edmund has spent many years of his life and out of prisons

Jack   That tends to be how the criminal justice system in this country works, yes

Esther   And is now missing.

Jack   Missing in what sense.

Esther   Nobody knows where he is.

Jack   Presumably, He knows where he is.

Esther   You've written about him quite extensively

Jack   I have?

Esther   You have

Jack   It's difficult for me to say – I'm not able to be objective

Esther   He was arrested for a series of murders and the book that. Made you Famous, that Broke Through – if we can use that kind of language

Jack   You just did

Esther   That book is all about Edmund

Jack   It's about many things

Esther   That book is all about Edmund

Jack   Is it?

Esther   Yes.

Jack   Okay.

Esther   You don't disagree

Jack   That's how you Received it, that's not for me to disagree with.

.

Esther   What do you think about Marlow's politics.

Jack   I don't.

Esther   You don't Agree with them or you don't think about them?

Anna   Jesus

Jack   I don't tend to think about them but when I Do think about them, yeah, I suppose I don't think Much of them I think that they are Poison but then he and I haven't been close since we were kids and he seems happy and.

.

You see this is why this is Hard for me – I'm not being deliberately Obstructive

Esther   Okay

Anna   You're not being obstructive enough

Timothy   right

Jack   It's just that This Process – Your Process – invites negativity and that's something we Consciously reject so.

.

Esther   I interviewed Marlow.

Jack   I know.

Esther   He's very dismissive of you.

Jack   I know.

Esther   How do you feel about that?

Jack   Do you Like his politics?

Esther   .

No.

Jack   I think I feel that he is poison and I don't want poison.

.

Esther   Did you Intend for the house to become This?

Jack   This?

Esther (*smiling, not infuriated, but struggling*)   Yes – *this*

Jack   And what is This

Esther   Your words. A Community. A Family.

.

Jack   No.

.

Esther   Well, then.

How did it happen?

Jack   .

People just. Started coming.

Maybe in response to some of the things that I had written, some of the ways in which I was talking about what it means to be Here, to be Alive I.

I decided to be Open.

Esther   .

Is it sexual?

Jack   It can be.

Esther   .

Can you say more about that?

Anna   Why.

You wanna watch us fuck?

Esther   Not particularly.

Anna   You wanna join in?

Esther   No

Anna   I think you do.

I think you're getting wet just Thinking about it.

Esther   Do they mind you writing about Them?

Jack writes About you all with quite a lot of detail

Anna (*to a camera*)   Does he, oh noooo

Esther   Can you – Does that Bother you? Do you read it?

Timothy   Why all the fucking questions.

Jack   She's making a documentary. Questions are fairly central to her process.

Is that fair?

Esther *nods.*

Esther   You don't like questions?

Timothy   They're like a machine gun. You're not really here. And no one asks the right ones.

Everyone thinks they're being really fucking insightful but you're just putting all this shit all this Air all of your own opinions all these Walls in between you and another person. It's fucking exhausting.

Esther   .

Okay.

Timothy   Just talk.

Esther   .

Okay.

Timothy   Just Be.

Esther   .

Okay.

Timothy   Just Do.

Esther   I think I get it.

Timothy (*smiling*)   Yeah I'm not sure you do.

Lucy *and* **Benny** *drift in at some point.* **Benny** *gets a beer. At some point* **Jack** *starts to barbecue the rabbit. The salad and the potatoes make their way to the table. At some point they start to eat and drink. They all start interacting with the cameras a bit more.*

Lucy (*to a camera*)   Helloooooo

.

Esther   I

Would you mind being careful they're very – I've set them up in a really specific. I. It's fine.

I

It feels. A bit. Can I say this?

Jack   Let's see

Esther   Okay, I feel

Weird – I feel like I'm Pissing you all off

.

I mean you did.

Invite me here.

Jack   So therefore you can do whatever you want to us

Esther   No. That's absolutely not what I

Jack   You can provoke and tease and bully and antagonise

Esther   If that's

how I'm coming Across then

Jack   I think it was a Mutual invitation, no

Esther   Well, I

Jack   You asked to speak to me about my work, I asked that
we could do that here – that you could see what we do Here

Esther   Yes, and I'm very grateful

Jack   So maybe you can do what you want to us and we can
do whatever we want to You.

From nearby – a **Man** *screams. Only* **Esther** *seems alarmed.*

.

Lucy   You know it's a very powerful feeling to just Submit.

.

Esther   That's not.

I'm not Here for.

.

I.

Wanted to ask about some of the Rituals that you guys have
but I Um

I'm Sensing

.

That Questions are not.

Another scream.

Sorry – is that

A beat. They all look to **Jack**.

Jack   Is what?

Esther   I heard. Someone.

Jack   Someone?

Esther   Someone screaming

Jack   .

I didn't. Did anyone else?

Lucy/Timothy/Anna/Benny   No.

A beat. Okay. They're fucking with her.

.

Esther   Maybe I should go

Jack   Why

Esther   I just

Jack   You're feeling uncomfortable

Esther   .

A bit.

Jack   Why d'you think that is.

.

Esther   I mean. This feels. And. I can hear someone screaming I

Jack   My experience in the creative process is that when shit gets Uncomfortable, it's beginning to get Real, I'm beginning to hit on something interesting.

It has to Cost something. The Making. Right?

.

Esther   [right]

.

Occasionally, we can hear the **Man** *screaming.*

Jack   What if we reverse it. Just for this evening. We'll ask Esther the questions.

Lucy   Fun

Benny   Who's Esther

Esther   Hi

Benny   Still no clearer poppet

Esther   I um I'm – making a film about Jack about your Home – none of you can Hear that?

Lucy   She's the Documentarian

Benny   Oh right

Jack   What d'you think

Esther   Is that a question

Jack   Ha

Esther   No, I mean. Yeah. Okay.

Anna   What happens if she fucks up

Jack   If she asks a question?

Anna   Yeah

Esther   Well I'll.

Try really hard not to

Anna   There still has to be a punishment – a consequence

Esther   Is that how things happen here?

Anna   That was a fucking question which means I get to Cut you

Esther   Then I'm not playing

Jack   No punishments.

We're all friends, this can be friendly.

Anna   Me first

Jack   Friendly

Anna   Who the fuck are you and what's your fucking problem

Jack   Anna, if we're opening with hostility then

Anna   Sorry

Jack   You don't need to apologise

Anna   Sorry

Jack   We sometimes need to adjust

Anna   Sorry

Jack (*with kindness*)   Enough.

Forgive yourself.

I love you.

Anna   Thank you, Jack.

.

Timothy   Why do you make documentaries.

Esther   Um.

I mean. I want to say because it helps me understand the world, but, truthfully. My father made documentaries and. Yeah.

Jack   You sound ashamed of that?

Esther   Um.

Maybe?

It would be

Bolder, right to. Just. Find what you're supposed to do and Step into it. Step where no man has stepped before. Not just. Copy your Dad.

Jack   I think there's something beautiful about acknowledging inspiration. Particularly if it came from your father

Esther   Why particularly

Anna   Fucking question can I Bite her

Esther   I'm sorry – ignore me

.

Benny   Okay I have one

Esther   Uh huh

Benny   Who actually Are you? Why Are you here?

Esther   Sure.

I'm Esther Lucas.

I've read Everything that Jack Roman has ever written and. I want to believe in it.

Lucy   What's stopping you.

Esther   I don't know.

Lucy   Why do you want to believe it?

Esther   Because.

It Feels true.

It Feels. Nihilistic. And. Yet. Strangely hopeful *because* of that. And. I think that's how I feel about the world.

Lucy   So.

What is stopping you.

Esther   .

Me?

Timothy   Question

Esther   Well, yeah, because I suppose it feels like that's what you Want me to say, you Want me to say I'm stopping myself

Timothy   Uh huh

Esther   But, honestly

Jack   Good

Esther   Maybe it feels

Male

Jack   Say more

Esther   Maybe your writing feels like it speaks to the Male experience of the world and that has Dominated for the last Forever, honestly

Jack   The Male Voice has

Esther   Yes, the male voice has dominated

Anna   What does that even *mean*

Esther   Well, it means exactly what it sounds like it means – you can't explain the Comet beyond Look Up and then a frustration that I cannot see what you see and I can't explain that the Male Voice has dominated just fucking Look Up and Notice that

Jack   I can hear someone screaming

Esther   Okay

Jack   But I wanted you to have the experience of people Doubting something that you are Certain about

Esther   Okay

Jack   And how did it feel

Esther   Infuriating

Jack   Exactly

Esther   Who is screaming

Jack   Question

Esther   Feels like a valid one

Jack   None of your questions are valid

Esther   Why is there a man Screaming his head off in your house and none of you are doing anything about it does feel like a valid question

Jack   Maybe there should be punishments.

Do you like the rabbit.

Esther   I do.

Jack   Why.

Esther   It tastes of grass.

Benny   When was the last time you swam

Esther   Um

I can't remember, I don't really like it

Lucy   Do you feel In your body

Esther   I

I don't know

Lucy   You don't look like you are

Esther   No?

Lucy   All shoulders

Esther   okay

Lucy   You look very anxious

Esther   Yes

I think I probably Am quite an anxious person

Timothy   Would you like to be Less anxious

Esther   Yes?

Lucy   You don't know?

Esther   No, I think I Don't know What I want

Lucy   You don't even know if you want to be less anxious

Esther   Well, that Sounds good that Sounds like something I should want I'm just Quite a Disconnected person I suppose

Jack   Why do you think that is?

Esther   .

I don't know

Jack   Why does my work mean so much to you.

A beat. She finds that difficult for some reason. She is surprised that that is difficult. He looks at her as though he understands. Kind. Allowing.

Esther   I.

Felt.

So completely understood when I read your books for the first time.

I felt.

I *feel*.

As though I understand my purpose and.

My Place in the world. and.

All of humanity, all of its history but.

But then.

But. Then.

James *comes on. He sort of ranges around, screaming occasionally, holding his head, crouching on the floor – in distress. He has some blood on him. Again, only* **Esther** *is alarmed.*

Esther   Um – Is he –

Are you – Is anyone –

Timothy   Do you take drugs, Esther

Esther   I don't really Know what you're Doing I – he seems – hello

Jack   This is James – can you answer Timothy's question

Esther   Hello

Jack   Timothy – again

Timothy   Do you take drugs, Esther

Esther   Uhhh I have done – have you hurt yourself

Timothy   Which ones

Esther   Can you Help him

Jack   We are helping him, we love him

All (*apart from* **Esther** *and* **Jack**)   We love you, James

At some point **James** *comes and rests his head in* **Jack***'s lap.* **Jack** *strokes his hair like he is a child or a dog.*

Esther   I think he needs

Timothy   Which drugs have you taken

Esther   This is

In my life?

Timothy   Yes

Esther   Uh. Weed? I don't

Timothy   Doesn't count

Esther   Can you hear me? What's wrong with him?

Jack   James is suffering

Esther   I can See that

Jack   You are looking

Anna   Look Up

Jack   James is In Pain

Esther   I can see that

Jack   We're Allowing James to feel whatever he needs to feel

Esther   I think James might need some Actual Help

Jack   What would you advise

Esther   Something more. Medical

James *barks.*

Anna   Fucking doctors.

Jack   That wouldn't be a good idea for James.

James is in the process of Submitting.

Esther   .

What does that mean.

James *rolls on the floor. They watch him. He laughs, ends up on his back with his legs in the air.*

James   Would you Like to try some other drugs?

Some laughter.

Esther   Um.

Sure. Maybe.

James *crawls to* **Esther**. *A big smile. All is okay.*

James   Sometimes I feel Overwhelmed.

Esther   .

James   Sometimes I feel like I can't cope.

Esther   Okay.

James   Do you ever feel like that?

Esther *nods*.

James   Sometimes I need to turn into a dog. Be treated like a dog.

Esther *nods*.

James   Sometimes, I think I understand my position in the world, in the community, I feel very Clear about everything, in fact, and then I step Into it, I step InTo the world and it is such a disappointment, or perhaps it is me that is the disappointment and I feel so Angry and so Panicked and so Afraid and Hopeless about the world and my place in it – I am both not enough and far too much and – do you ever feel like that Esther

Esther   how do you know my name

James   I knew that I would see you – do you ever feel like that

Esther   Yes.

James (*very gentle, very loving*)   We take LSD.

Esther   Okay.

James   D'you know what that is?

Esther   Uh

Yeah.

I've heard of it.

James   It comes from the earth

Esther   Okay

James   We call it Mother

Esther   Mother?

James   Yeah.

She's gonna wrap her arms around you and take you back to the beginning and let you rebuild.

Jack's our guide. He'll take care of you.

Esther *shakes her head slightly.*

Esther   I.

James   Please.

Esther   .

James   Hold my hand.

She does.

.

Jack   Don't forget to look up.

.

They take LSD.

It feels like a ritual.

There's music, it feels gentle and like sliding into a trip – Mica Levi's Jackie *score is a good reference.*

The sky fills with stars. It's beautiful.

And then the music shifts into something more frenetic. And then it's a party and they're dancing.

And then someone is singing.

Something like 'Ghost Rider' by Suicide.

And they're dancing and they're kissing each other and it's all love, everything is love.

Jack   You're safe.

Esther   Oh.

Jack   No more questions.

Esther   Oh.

Jack   This is where you're supposed to be.

Esther   Oh.

.

I'm tiny.

I don't exist yet.

It's the beforetimes.

I'm walking across a sheet of black ice and the sky above me is black and I don't need to worry about before I was here nothing that happened has anything to do with me I don't need to care about it anymore I don't need to care about my place in history and

I'm warm and I'm wet and I'm back in the womb

I can hear a Rush of sound loud like the sea but I don't know what the sea Is yet I'm in water and I'm sucking and I'm So safe, This is the safest I will ever feel and as I head towards the birth canal, because it is time, because if I don't then it will mean death, I realise that this is the Greatest grief, the Deepest loss I will ever experience and if I can manage This then I will be fine, I am in my cot and the bars are cold and I am crying and my Mother is sitting cross-legged on the floor in front of me and She is crying too because she is tired and she cannot make it better and she didn't get to experience the grief of my birth because everyone was so terribly focused on telling her that becoming a Mother was going to be the making of her and now that I Know that now that I have been given the opportunity to Relive that and to Witness that with adult eyes I can forgive her, I can forgive her everything and that is Peaceful that is Full of Peace that could change the World in the future will everyone do this will everyone travel to South America and do this will everyone sit in Conference centres in Birmingham that have been decorated with plants and fairy lights and incense sticks whilst a man named Chad who shaved his head and spent time with the shamans in Peru is now standing in front of you, mixing you tea, helping you purge – he's going to take you on a guided trip so that you can head Inwards further Inwards further Inwards and make discoveries about yourself and then come back and tell everybody else to go and do it tell everybody else to head further inwards That will save the world and I am Four and I am watching my Father Run across a dance floor with a camera in his hand, watching my father run through the Streets with a camera in his hand, watching my Mother cry and rock on the floor and my Father's response is to raise his camera and point it At Her, I am Ten and a man who insists that I call him Uncle despite him being of no relation is removing his dressing gown in front of me on the landing at the top of the stairs and asking if I want to touch his I am Twelve and I am kissing a boy and our teeth are banging together and he's grabbing at what will hopefully grow into a left tit one day I am fifteen and I am reading a book by Jack Roman whilst planes fly overhead and I am Altered I can feel my Insides Physically Alter I am reading I am reading I am reading I start to read poems his wife wrote in a Sanatorium and I read him again and he has ruined Sex and Love for me forever because nothing could ever feel That Good nothing will ever Fuck Me like his books Fuck Me I read his wife's memoirs and I feel bored and betrayed I read the feminist criticism and I wonder if they should just get laid I reread his first book and fall asleep and it is Lazy, it is funny and confident but it is Lazy and I fuck an Actual Man and it is actually not That bad maybe I will try that again I am seventeen and my Grandma has died and everyone is sobbing and Men are going to war Men are going to war and I am wondering whether she has left me any money or perhaps a diamond ring old people have diamond rings don't they and I am nineteen and my father is telling me I don't have a point of view I don't have an opinion how do I expect to Make anything if I don't have the courage to take a Perspective on anything I am twenty-two and I reread Jack

Roman and I read Clarissa Castorp and I feel things I had
not felt and my Mother is trying to hug me and I am
shrugging her off because I find her grotesque women past
the age of forty are fucking grotesque even though I Know
what she did for me I Know what her body went through for
me she should still have had the grace to Step Off the Earth
once she hit Forty I am twenty-seven and I am dancing but I
am not in my body and I do not know how to get there I am
tired I am exhausted I do not know what I want to Say but I
know that I want to say Something that it will feel good to
say Something maybe if I come here I will be able to say
Something without actually having to Say Something I am
here now everything has led to Here Now and I am looking
up and I see A Comet.

All (*they speak in unison apart from* **Jack** *who stands centre stage
looking up*)   I see A Comet.

Hurtling Across the sky.

The sky was black a moment ago but now it is blue.
Aquamarine.

Pink.

White hot light, a ball and a tail, just as you might have
imagined if somebody Asked you to imagine a comet.

It is heading towards us.

Who knows how long until it hits. But one day it will.

We have given up.

Surrendered ourselves to somebody who

Jack   It Is coming, isn't it.

You can see it, can't you.

All (*apart from* **Jack**)   I don't know.

We see what you tell us to see.

Jack   Well, don't. Look Up. Look Up.

All (*apart from* **Jack**)   We do.

We just have Your eyes.

Part Four

AUTUMN

Jack *and* **Miranda** *are in a garden area of a restaurant. He is sitting. She is standing.*

Miranda   I don't know why I'm here yet.

Jack   .

Okay.

Miranda   I don't know if I'm gonna stay.

Jack   Okay.

That's fine.

.

Would you like to sit down whilst you figure that out or

Miranda   No

Jack   Okay.

That's fine.

Miranda   I don't need you to say that.

Jack   No, of course you don't.

.

Miranda   I want to look at you but I also really fucking don't want You to look at me looking at you I don't want to be Observed.

Jack   Okay

Miranda   Could you look Up or look over there or just don't look at me

Jack   Okay

Miranda   Could you Stop saying okay

Jack   .

Yes.

.

She looks at him.

Miranda (*upset*)   Fuck.

A **Waitress** *comes over.*

Waitress   Hi there

Miranda   hi

Waitress   Can I take your coat

Miranda   No.

Waitress   .

Uh. Okay. Can I get you guys anything to drink

Miranda   I'm not sure if I'm staying yet

Waitress   .

Okay. Um.

Have you guys eaten here before?

Miranda   No   **Jack**   No.

Waitress   Um, it's like the menu is sort of   .

designed to be sharing plates   .

Miranda   Of course it fucking is how terribly original

Waitress   Uh.

Yeah, so I'd recommend like maybe three or four of the smaller plates and then two from the mains and um maybe a side

Jack   Thank you

Waitress   Um.

And uh did you want to hear our specials or should I come back

Miranda   Yes.

Waitress   I should come back

Miranda   No, tell us the specials, I love hearing the specials.

The **Waitress** *does not know if* **Miranda** *is being serious.*

Miranda   Go.

Waitress   Um.

We have a pan-roasted pigeon breast with. Sorrel and. Bacon.

And a trout with a garlic lemon butter sauce or a

Braised rabbit pappardelle with foraged wild mushrooms

Miranda   Those all sound genuinely incredible

Waitress Yeah the um, the rabbit looks amazing

Miranda I'm a vegetarian

Waitress .

Right, yes.

Miranda Can I get some water please with a lot of ice

Waitress Sure

Miranda And no, like, citrus or cucumber or Flowers or anything in it okay

Waitress Okay

The **Waitress** *leaves.*

Jack How long have you been a vegetarian

Miranda I'm not.

I just wanted to make her feel bad.

.

Jack I read your book on the way here.

Miranda .

Jack   The new one.

Miranda   Okay.

Jack   I thought it was

Miranda   I don't need to hear your opinion.

I haven't asked for it, I haven't invited it.

Jack   .

Well.

You Wrote something.

Isn't that an invitation for

Anybody to read it

Miranda   I don't think of it that way.

Jack   No?

Miranda   No.

Jack   I always felt it was a dialogue. Between myself and the reader, I was

Extending a.

An Idea, an Offering of some kind and.

And I was always.

Very moved that there was a response.

Miranda   Okay, well.

That's a lovely load of bullshit you've fed yourself but that's not really how it works for me.

It's not a Gift for the world

Jack   No, that's not what I meant

Miranda   I don't care what anyone thinks about it, I wrote it for myself.

Jack   Sure, but then

Miranda   Then what

Jack   Well. Why Publish it. You have to acknowledge that the thing that was Just for you is now being Offered to the world

Miranda   I don't have to acknowledge anything I don't agree with your theory, that might be how You wrote Your books but that's not how I feel about my work.

Jack   Okay, well. I would like to tell you that I thought it was Really interesting

Miranda   I've been shortlisted for the Booker I don't need you to tell me you found it Interesting.

Are you gonna get your Pulitzer out?

The **Waitress** *returns with a jug of water with lots of ice and two glasses. She puts it down on the table.* **Miranda** *is still standing.*

Waitress   Our water is fresh from a spring and we import our ice from the Arctic

Miranda   Wow

Waitress   I know

Jack   Is that ethical

Miranda   I'm not sure you should be using that word – Can I get the pigeon and a vodka martini please.

Waitress   .

Uh.

Yes, absolutely.

Um.

That Is. Just so you. That does have Meat in it, it's not.

The chef wouldn't recommend it. As being Suitable for. Vegetarians.

Miranda   .

Amazing.

.

Jack   I'll have the soup, please.

The **Waitress** *leaves.*

Miranda   The soup

Jack   Uh huh

Miranda   Do you have gout

Jack   Uhhhh.

No. Not got that one yet.

Miranda   Looks like it might be coming for you any day now

Jack   Okay then, well.

Thank you for the heads-up.

Miranda   I'm still not sure if I'm staying.

Jack   I understand.

Miranda   I think.

I wanted to see how Small you were.

.

Jack   And?

Miranda   Very.

You are a Very Diminished.

Small.

Man.

.

You Look small on the television.

I've been watching you. Dragging yourself all around the Breakfast shows and doing the Interviews and writing the Apologetic think pieces and staring into your camera on your laptop with your head slight Tilted saying you're Really Sorry for all the Hurt you caused

Jack   Well, I fucked up

Miranda   You got cancelled.

And you want to get UnCancelled. You want your seat back at the table.

Jack   I understand why it looks that way but I really don't.

I was in a position of power

Miranda   Oh good I'm gonna get the live version

Jack   And I abused it.

The **Waitress** *brings the martini over. She puts it down on the table along with a basket of bread and a bowl of tomatoes.*

Waitress   Ummm, some sourdough and an anchovy and tomato tapenade just to get you started and.

Enjoy.

The **Waitress** *leaves.* **Miranda** *looks at the drink. They don't eat the bread.*

Jack   Are you Drinking again

Miranda   .

Considering it.

.

Jack   Is that a.

Miranda   No, it's a terrible idea.

It would derail my life and be a huge betrayal to those who love me – which is many people by the way, there are Many people who love me.

Jack   I'm glad to hear that. I only Wanted you to have Love in your life.

Miranda   But not from my father.

.

She picks up the drink and downs it.

(*Calling out to the* **Waitress**.) Can I get another

Drinks keep arriving and she keeps drinking them.

She sits down.-

You don't really believe that shit you have to keep saying do you.

Abuse of power. Terrible harm.

Jack   Yes.

Of course I do.

Miranda   But you didn't do anything That bad.

Jack   Well.

The people who were There, who. Lived in that house with me. During that time. They feel otherwise.

Miranda   So what. Your whole career has to be Re-evaluated because someone has Hurt feelings.

No one's accusing you of anything

Physical

Jack   No.

Miranda   You didn't Lock people in rooms or hold them against their will.

Jack   No.

Miranda   You just told a bunch of fucked-up people that you had the answers and then it turned out you didn't and they got mad.

.

And.

What are we supposed to Do with you anyway now?

All of your work with a little Content Warning on it – but what about You, the Person – what do we Do with you, what are you Supposed to do, I never understand what we're saying about humanity – you know, you Wrote some stuff, you said some shit, you were trying to find yourself as an artist and then you Blew Up, right, you become this Cultural Phenomenon and the world Makes you something you weren't even Trying to be, everyone's Projecting what they Want you to be and then you Fuck up, okay, we can agree, some FuckUppery happens and we send you off to the Wilderness because you reminded us you were fallible and we thought you were God, right.

Jack   Well.

Maybe.

Yeah, I mean it's.

Been hard.

Being out in a sort of

Cultural Wasteland I.

Yeah.

.

Miranda   That was quick.

.

You've been out there Self-Flagellating all over the place, Begging forgiveness, Showing Contrition – you have the Best Contrition face I've ever seen – we play this Game when we're Doing you at home and we do this – 'Remorse Remorse My Kingdom for Remorse' – *Writing* about it, writing about how much You've healed from Learning about what an abusive piece of shit you were and look you've just Given it all back in a second because I Flattered you and said it wasn't such a big deal – you caused people Enormous Fucking Harm it's not up for debate you should be in Fucking Prison.

.

Jack That's not.

Factually. Correct. I.

Look, through My own lack of clarity or Care over my language you have

Misinterpreted what I meant – but I will take a lesson from that, so thank you

Miranda Well that was almost Beautiful

Jack right

Miranda Masterful

Jack that's

Miranda Who does your Media Training I want her, I'm assuming it's a her, did you ever Imagine when you were little that you would have to be Media Trained by a woman with straw-coloured hair called Helen or Carol they're always called fucking Carol

Jack I don't

Miranda Where's My Fucking Apology.

.

Where's my Parade of Sorrys.

Why aren't you standing in front of Microphones apologising for what you did to Me?

Jack   I am sorry.

I am sorry that I was So absent from your life. It is my Greatest regret.

Miranda   Well, I don't believe a word that comes out of your fucking mouth.

I don't have children.

Jack   No.

Miranda   You showed me that Nothing is more important than the work. So.

I am grateful for that

Jack   I have caused you pain. And I am sorry for that.

Miranda (*upset*)   You haven't caused me pain.

You haven't done anything to me.

You've not got in.

I hope you've noticed that I Never write about you.

You're a Chasm.

You are a Void.

You are a Nothing.

.

Jack   I.

I'm.

(*to her or to the audience – a sort of smile*) I'm struggling to

Know what to say at this point

Miranda (*also maybe not as* **Miranda** *anymore, maybe this is the actor*)   Yeah?

Jack (*is this* **Jack** *or the actor?*)   Yeah, I'm.

I'm genuinely not sure how to

Respond.

Miranda Uh huh.

Should we just. Sit here for a bit?

See what happens?

They sit there. Maybe they eat, maybe they don't – but they do stay there together. They watch the next scene as though they are in the audience for it. They find it funny.

A podcast studio. **Marlow** *sits with two guys –* **Patrick** *and* **Joe**. *A lot of neon signs, stripped-down wooden coffee table, massive comfortable leather sofa, big headphones, good mics, cameras filming them, tight T-shirts. *Lots* of sound effects and jingles played throughout – a polished, produced show.* **Johnny** *sits behind a laptop, hitting the keys for the jingles/noises.*

Patrick   Heeeeeeey what is up what is up

Joe   How are you guys

Patrick   It is a Beautiful day

Joe   It is

Patrick   And you know Why it is beautiful, Joe, my friend

Joe   Why, Patrick, Why is it such a beautiful day

Patrick   Because we are here recording today's Pod with a Such a fucking Legend

Joe   Content Warning

Patrick   Content Warnings Get Fucked, joining us today on In Deep is – Honestly, I cannot overstate this

Joe   Couldn't even if you tried

Patrick   He's Honestly the reason I feel like I'm even here, he's Such an Inspiration

Joe   Alright don't get your Period, man

Patrick   I know I feel like I'm one of those, like, Sobbing Ozempic Bitches in my Dress holding my Gold dildo thanking My Agent and then thanking God second, *thank you sooooo much for making me a whore*

Joe   Sit Down, Bitch

Patrick   Marlow Fucking Roman

Joe   MARLOW fucking Roman

Marlow   What's up, guys

Patrick   Honestly, man

Joe (*miming giving the microphone a blow job*)   Thank you for making Patty's dreams come true

Marlow   Good to be here

Patrick   I feel like we barely gave you an intro there

Joe   That's cos you were reading your teenage diary out

Patrick   I mean obviously, we talk about you All the fucking time on In Deep

Joe   All the Fucking *Time*

Patrick   So our listeners are like *Super*-familiar with you and your work and just like everything that you've been doing since you were – honestly, you got started so young, right

Marlow   Uh huh.

.

Yeah.

I was out in the world, getting my hands dirty from pretty young – as soon as I finished school really.

Patrick   And, like, not a foot wrong since then – you've just been Empire building

Marlow   Uh huh

Patrick   Like, your own Personal little fucking Empire

Marlow   Uh huh

Joe   Was that always the ambition?

Marlow   What?

Patrick   Be specific, man, that was such a vague fucking question

Joe   I'm sorry, man, I cannot hear you on account of your head being All the way up Marlow's fucking ass – yeah, I mean, you're at the Top right

Marlow   I'm at the top

Joe   You have been in the Top Five Richest men in the world for, like, the last – it feels like centuries – but it's Consistent

Patrick   Men and Women, Joe

Joe   Oh yes, sorry, excuse me, Top Five Richest People in the world

Patrick   Except it is Literally All men

Marlow   I have been near the number one spot since I started or since the lists started or whatever, yeah

Joe   And was that always the Ambition

Marlow   To be at The Top?

Joe   Yeah

Marlow   No, I wanted to be mediocre and this is all just a fucking Accident

Patrick   buuuuurn

Joe   OUCH

Marlow   I guess that Is how most people in the world operate – aim for mediocrity and hit just below it, but no, I was ambitious from pretty young, yeah

Joe   And you've got this Beautiful family

Marlow   Uh huh

Joe   The Lovely Rosa

Marlow   Yes

Patrick   And you guys have Eight children?

Marlow   We have Eight children, exactly, and I have Ten children by other women and I'm Incredibly close to All of my children

Joe   Incredible

Patrick   Inspirational

Joe   Amazing

Patrick   That feels like such a Thing, right – Men being Close to their Children

Joe   Pcccccccdo

Marlow   The fuck are you doing, do you Know what you're saying?

Patrick   I guess *I* wonder. Like. Uh. Yeah. Has that ever been like. I mean.

Has Rosa ever been like. You know – all respect to Lady Rosa, she's a Legend in her own right

Marlow   She is

Patrick   Like, Amazing Mum, so Supportive of you, she's The most followed Content Creator on, like, fucking everything, I can't even list and you know, she gets it, keep shit smooth at home and let you go out and be Wild, be what You need to be

Marlow   Exactly

Patrick   But I guess what I'm asking is, like, has she ever given you shit or been like – about those other women

Marlow   No.

Why would she.

What grounds would she Possibly have.

Keep my home clean.

Put food on my table.

Raise my kids to be Honourable, Hard Working, Morally Upright – and you know, guys, it's not like I'm making that Hard for her – we've got fucking chefs and maids and nannies all over the place, the other day there's this Guy in my Beach House kitchen right and he's watering these Ficus plants – and he's looking at me kind of funny and his hands shaking and I'm like, come on, get it together

Patrick   He's me, he's me – that guy is Absolutely Me

Marlow   And I look at him and I'm like who the fuck are you – cos, I've got to be careful right, I am a Target, you know how many assassination attempts I've survived

Joe   Right

Marlow   Do you?

Joe   Uh

Marlow   I'm Asking You

Joe   Like, Four

Marlow   Actual shots Fired – Seven – And he can barely speak, his little high-pitched squeaky voice just goes – oh, sir, sorry, sir – dribbling all over the place and I'm really thinking okay in a second I'm gonna Have to whip my dick out to wipe all this Saliva up – and he goes, oh, sir, I'm the Ficus Guy

Patrick   The Ficus guy

Marlow   Exactly

Joe   Who's the Ficus Guy

Marlow   My Wife has Hired some guy to water Just the Ficus plants in the Beach House – which, is, to be clear, just a little like fucking Annexe on a property – that's literally his only job and I'm paying him something like a 100k a year I am Not kidding you guys so yeah, my wife's good, I get her diamonds, I get her what she wants, she doesn't give me shit – I'm looking after her, she's looking after me – that's how it works in the world, no? Like, I know you've got some Macho spin on it and I get it, I agree with some of your sentiments – Not all of them, I might add, I think little boys like you should Wash your fucking mouths out – you think talking into your little microphones and lifting a kettle bell and pressing a little button on your Noise Machine makes you a fucking Man, you know how many people I have literally Decapitated to get to where I am – but look, essentially, we're on this planet to make Connections with other people, right? Work together. Make something bigger that ourselves, leave something behind.

You gonna cry dipshit?

They laugh and then they turn and look at/run to – the following scene.

Edmund *who is in a village hall.* **Miranda** *and* **Jack** *watch him as well. He's waiting. And then he is joined by* **Thomas** *and* **Tommy**. *Wellies, anoraks sort of vibe.* **Johnny** *begins to move between all three scenes – observing, engaging with each with a slightly different energy. Is he being the actor more than the characters here?*

Edmund Fantastic.

Brilliant.

Okay, I think this is probably Us – I've been running these workshops for a number of years now and actually Two is a Great number to be working with for an introductory session. As you start to progress then a larger group can work really well and can feel really

Exciting actually, but that's something to build up to, and, if this works for you and you feel like you've Found something here then this really could be the start of your new life.

.

So.

Before we get started, why don't we do names –

Thomas   Hi, I'm Thomas

Edmund   Fantastic

Tommy   That's funny

Edmund   Yes

Is it

Tommy   No it's just – I'm Tommy

Thomas   Oh

Edmund   Right

Tommy   Thomas and Tommy

Edmund   Yes

Tommy   I guess we've got a fair bit in common

Edmund   Yes

Tommy   The fact we're here

Edmund   Yes

Tommy   And our names

Edmund   Yes.

.

Tommy   I wonder if there's other stuff

Johnny   Hi

Edmund   Hello

Johnny   Knock knock

Tommy   Are you Tommo

Johnny   'scuse me

Tommy   Another TomTom to add to the mix

Edmund   No he's

Johnny   This is my hall

Tommy   Oh

Johnny   I run the hall

Tommy   Got it

Johnny   Just checking you're all good

Edmund   Yes thanks

Johnny   Got the keys

Edmund   Yep

Johnny   You'll run through the fire safety

Edmund   Yeah, we did that

Johnny   Nice one stay safe out there –

Edmund   Thanks, Johnny –

Johnny *leaves this scene and puts on a chef's hat, chef's whites, he goes to the restaurant table where he picks up the tomato tapenade and smears it all over his clothes.* **Miranda** *and* **Jack** *help him, they find it funny – is that enough, oh shit –*

Edmund   So I'm Edmund

Tommy   Hello, Edmund

Edmund   And I guess to kick us off it would be great to hear a bit about what brought you both here today – Tommy, why don't you kick us off

Tommy   Absolutely, yeah. I mean. I'm a pretty Adventurous sort of guy

Edmund   Uh huh

Tommy   I've always felt like I'm just a very Open person, I'm just very Open to new experiences

Edmund   Fantastic

Tommy   I saw this flyer in uh a pub when I was on this Walking holiday – for your group, for this workshop – and I was just like. Yeah. Count me in. Sign Me Up.

Edmund   That's great, thank you for sharing – Thomas, how about you?

Thomas   Uh.

I had a breakdown about seven months ago.

Edmund   Okay.

.

I'm sorry to hear that

Thomas   Did you want me to elaborate

Edmund   I mean – only if You wanted to

Thomas   I couldn't walk.

There was nothing wrong with me Physically, I just couldn't move my legs and the doctors didn't know why – nobody knew why and. I had a lot of time to think.

.

I hate the world.

I hate what's happened to the world.

.

I hate all of it.

I hate the Politics and the Shops and the Money and the Stuff and all of the boxes that keep firing through the door and hitting the floor and I hate the way we eat. I hate supermarkets. I hate being overwhelmed by everything and exhausted by everything but I hate that that's all that people Talk about now that we all say God isn't it awful standing in a shop trying to choose a sandwich or what to watch on television or where to go on your holidays – but aren't we lucky, aren't we Lucky that we are the ones that have the opportunity to be Overwhelmed by choice, well, I don't feel lucky, I feel like human beings are Stupid and disgusting and we have made Awful decisions for centuries now and we Stink, we all Reek. The disappointment is overwhelming.

.

Edmund   Thank you, Thomas

Tommy   Wow

Thomas   Sorry

Edmund   No

Thomas   That was too much

Edmund   No, it was.

Look, it's exactly why I'm here too.

And I find that You being here, and You being here, Tommy, I find that enormously hopeful.

.

Did you have an animal in mind?

Thomas   Well.

I like the idea of a Fox.

Edmund   Fantastic.

An urban fox or a rural fox

Thomas   I think – maybe just to Start with – as a transition, I was thinking Urban fox

Edmund   I think that's really smart – Tommy, how about you

Tommy   Um I mean. I liked what you talked about on the leaflet – you were a Badger

Edmund   I was a badger for a while, yes

Tommy   Yeah, I feel like I could do badger, I feel sort of Drawn to that – though I don't know why

Edmund   Instincts are So important, Tommy, it's really all about tuning into your Instinct rather than that voice that pipes up and starts questioning everything you do

Tommy   Okay great then yeah I'd love to start with badger

Edmund   Brilliant – and I'm actually going to be a fox to start with

Tommy   Oh

Edmund   Just because badgers are a little more Dominant than foxes

Tommy   Oh?

Edmund   Particularly an Urban fox – but I will move into Badger at some point during the exercise, and, if we're all Open

Tommy   Uh huh

Edmund   You're both going to just Observe that transition

Thomas   Okay

Edmund   And so, in a minute, I'm going to ask you both to take your jackets off and to get down onto the floor and onto all fours – and once we do that, we're acknowledging that we're leaving our human selves behind, okay?

.

It will take us a little while and we won't shed these human parts immediately – you've been living in them your whole lives so I want you to be kind to yourself, give yourself a lot of grace.

.

And we won't leave language fully behind. For these first few hours we'll communicate verbally when we need to. And it's my job to keep you safe. Your stomach isn't badger yet, your stomach isn't fox – so uncooked chicken and roadside squirrel won't hit right quite yet, but we'll work up to it – probably with a few worms for you, Tommy, and a bit of light bin scavenging for you, Thomas, but I've been doing this for a while – living as an otter or a deer or a rabbit or a stoat – out in what I think of as the Real World, not the Fake World everyone else is concerned with and I promise you that it's going to be a really profound experience.

.

So, now. If you're ready, we're going to take off our jackets –

They do.

And we're going to get on all fours, and we're going to go out into the Real World as our animal selves. And we're gonna see what we become next.

.

Okay?

They do.

They crawl out of the room.

The sound of gunshots. **Marlow** *mimes firing a gun into the sky.* **Johnny** *comes back into the hall carrying the gun from Part One. He still has his chef's whites on, smeared in the tomato.*

.

Jack   I really don't know what to say.

Waitress (*bringing food over*)   The pigeon and the soup – and the chef's accompaniment

Jack   Oh

Miranda *starts tucking in immediately.*

Waitress   A little salad of endive, chicory, hazelnuts and from our smokery – fox haunch and badger loin

Jack   Oh

Waitress   Chef likes to really look at the choices you've made and then comes up with a very bespoke accompaniment

Miranda   It's really good

Waitress   Oh great

Miranda   Feels like it's just full of fucking Iron and

Waitress   Absolutely

Miranda   All the good shit

Waitress   Yeah, Chef is really into working with Roadkill and what we Find and

Miranda   That's so cool

Jack   I feel a little uh nauseous

Miranda   Didn't you do this shit all the time? When you were out there In The Wild

Johnny   Hope you're enjoying the food

Miranda   It's delicious

Johnny   Freshly shot

Miranda   Amazing

Johnny   Watch out for the pellets

Miranda   Will do

Johnny   They'll break your fucking teeth

Miranda   Right

Johnny   But then you know you're eating something Real, right

Jack   I mean

Johnny   We're not covering entrails in breadcrumbs and giving it a Cute fucking name, right, you're Consuming Life and you're Alive, right, this is It

Jack   Is it

Johnny   Would you like me to talk you through the process

Jack   No thank you

Miranda   Yes please!

Johnny   Once you've skinned it and removed the tail, chopped its head off, you need to open the sides of the sternum to take the windpipe out

Miranda   Yum Yum

Johnny   Cut the feet off at the ankles and get all the fur off – we use the fur to make our napkins – nice, aren't they

Miranda   Really special

Johnny   Open the chest cavity and remove all of the innards, slice up the diaphragm, clear the colon and then take out all of the shit

Miranda   Uh huh

Johnny   I'm talking about faecal matter

Miranda   I was wondering when somebody would

Johnny   Salvage all of the organs

Miranda   Naturally

Johnny   The organs are delicious

Jack   I feel a bit sick

Johnny   It's absolutely fantastic isn't it, it's Absolutely what we're supposed to be doing – I used to work in media, fucking nightmare

Johnny *picks up the jug of water from the table and goes to the ice baths and pours it in. He gives a cigar to* **Marlow**, *lights it for him.*

Miranda   What a genius

Waitress   Yeah, he's Amazing to work for

Miranda   This tastes like Grass

Waitress   In a good way

Miranda   It's the Only thing I want to eat

Jack   He's covered it in a Jus and a Foam and a Crumb and charged me £28 for it is that what it means to be alive

Waitress   I'm a really big fan of your work by the way

Jack   Thank you

.

Miranda   Thank you.

Marlow *goes and gets into an ice bath, cigar still in his mouth.*

Waitress   I mean.

She meant **Miranda**.

Waitress   Sorry, I meant.

I haven't read.

I'm not familiar with your work – I didn't know that you were a writer

Jack   It's fine

Miranda   You would Totally have heard of him – he's called Jack Roman

Waitress   Uhhhhhh

Miranda   He was uh Cancelled in a really major way a couple of years ago

Jack   I mean

Edmund *crawls back into the space.*

Waitress   Ohhhhhhh

He is followed by **Thomas** *and* **Tommy** *– all on all fours, sniffing around.*

Jack   Yeah it's just not that

Waitress   Right

Jack   Simple

Waitress   The cult guy

Miranda   Yes exactly

Waitress   Yeah I mean, I remember the whole

Story – you're a Writer?

I don't remember that – I just remember all the

Cult stuff

Miranda   Yeah the cult stuff was pretty

Memorable

Jack   .

Yeah.   **Edmund** *starts to stand, become his human self.*

Yeah, I'm a writer.

Waitress   Well.

(*To* **Miranda**.) I really love all your stuff – I love

how you write

about what it is to be a woman, about the

female experience

Jack   Do you?

Waitress   .

Yeah?

.

.

.

Jack   You didn't find it

.

.

Parochial?

.

.

Parochial means

having a Narrow Scope or outlook.

.

.

Edmund   Okay, that's wonderful.

.

Let's start to stand up, let's reconnect with our

Human

Selves again

.

Tommy, I want you to leave your Badger self behind

for now

.

Thomas, let go of your fox, leave him in the

wilderness, it's okay.

The men stand up. They look dazed.

.

Waitress Yeah, I know what it means.

.

That's not how it feels to read Miranda's work.

.

It feels Expansive.

.

Jack Uh huh

You know what, can I get a whiskey.

.

.

Waitress Sure.

Johnny *starts to play some kind of club music –*

for **Marlow***'s benefit. He's into it.*

.

The **Waitress** *leaves.*

.

How are you feeling?

.

Thomas Uh.

.

I feel. I think I feel really Sad?

Edmund Uh huh

.

Tommy Me too.

.

Edmund Well, that's okay.

That's a valuable thing to feel.

.

.

.

.

Jack   It's not that I find it parochial

Miranda   I don't care

Jack   I can just feel you

In the writing.

Stretching

Yearning for something Bigger

Miranda   No.

.

.

.

We can sit in that for a moment.

We can sit in the sadness. In the overwhelm.

Let's just Hold it for each other.

For ourselves.

.

.

.

.

Marianne *enters holding a lunchbox.*

Marianne   Hi!

Tommy   Oh

Marianne   Sorry to interrupt

Edmund   This is a private workshop – I've booked the hall

.

That's called projection.

.

The *Feeling* in the novel

.

Jack   Yes?

.

Miranda   What she *Feels*

Jack   Yes?

.

Miranda   I don't have to Explain my work
to you.

Jack   No, of course not.

.

Marianne   No it's just   **Tommy**   No, sorry, this is

.

He forgot his lunch, I just

.

Tommy   I told you we'd be eating.

.

Marianne   No, I know.

.

.

Tommy   I told you we'd be Hunting.

.

.

Marianne   No, of course, I.

It's just he'd said he might be an Otter or a Weasel or

Tommy   A badger, I told you, I was gonna be a

badger

Marianne   Okay, well, they eat things like. Like

Voles and um

Mice and

Edmund   This really isn't okay

Tommy   I'm really sorry

Thomas   I don't think I'd have come if I'd've known

This was gonna happen

Tommy   I'm really fucking sorry

Marianne   I just, I made some cheese and pickle

sandwiches just in case and

.

.

.

.

.

.

.

.

.

.

.

Miranda   Just because she isn't on top of a

mountain or in the ice or at Sea

or at War doesn't mean it isn't Enormous,

doesn't make it.

Domestic.

.

.

.

The **Waitress** *brings a whiskey and puts it down.*

Jack   Is there any way that that Music could

be turned down or

Waitress   Sorry

It's a private members' club next door, nothing

I can do about it.

.

Jack   Okay.

.

.

.

.

Look, I can throw it out there on the Grass or

something if it helps I just

.

She throws the lunchbox on the floor. They all look at it.

.

.

Marianne   I'm sorry.

.

.

I think I just.

.

Wanted to Look at you and See if this had Helped.

Edmund   Helped?

Marianne   Helped him be less sad.

Miranda   You look all sad.

Jack   Okay.

Miranda   You look like a scrunched-up bit

of paper.

Jack   Okay.

Miranda   Discarded and thrown aside.

Jack   Is that a line from one of your Books.

.

.

It sounds like a line from one of your books.

I wonder why you decided to become a writer

Miranda   I didn't Decide to Become

Jack   Oh you just Were

Miranda   Yes

Jack   You were just Called upon, it just

The tapping gets **Johnny** *to start stripping down to swimwear.*

He starts signalling to **Tommy** *and* **Thomas**.

Happened to be that way

Miranda   Yes

Jack   The Gods

Miranda   Yes

Jack   Nothing to do with me

Miranda   Nothing to do with you

Jack   *I* fucking

Decided.

.

I Decided.

.

.

I went out, and I Claimed it.

I Stepped into the World and I Grabbed it, I

Wrestled for it I

.

.

.

.

.

.

.

Johnny   Come on.

.

Tommy *starts to strip off too.* **Marianne** *watches, sad.*

Edmund *too.*

No one's surprised.

.

.

Made it possible

Miranda   Congratulations

Jack   Yes fucking congratulations, yes well done me – I Clawed at it I Carved at it I Fought for every word, for my career, for each experience and each story and I Made something from Nothing I made things Exist Where They Had Not Existed Before – and you get to just Drift along in the wake of that, Happily going by Miranda Roman, convincing yourself that the world is charmed by your lack of Speech Marks when a character is talking, Full of derision for My work yet Painfully Unaware of the fact that you would never have got a seat at the fucking table were it not for the Roman that sits at the end of your name – I'm *sorry* that I didn' plait your hair or sing you lullabies or kiss your grazed knees or attend Any of your birthday parties – I am, I *know* that by your generation's standards I was a Useless father and husband and friend and Human, but I was Attentive to the Blank Fucking Page and my own life in relation only to that, defining myself entirely on my own terms and that has made me Better that has made me Extraordinary that has made me – at times – Defining and don't we Want that don't we Crave that, isn't that Necessary and I have Lived I have Lived I have Lived and I am Owed something I am fucking Owed a World a nightly applause an armful of wildflowers a Swoon a Thank You I am not due this I am not due spooning thin soup into my mouth and my head stooped in an eternal apology because I Dared to Live Boldly, do you know that when I was ten years old my Mother died and I met my Uncle on the fields covered in another man's blood and he told me to go and seek life and adventure and I *did* and this paler version of the world is something I want no part of you are a terrible fucking writer.

Miranda *stares.*

Stands up as if to leave.

The **Waitress** *approaches.*

Waitress   Sorry. I just. You know. I write. A bit. .

.

I have a Substack.

Miranda   Okay.

Waitress   I'd love to send you a

Marlow *starts tapping an empty glass next to his ice*

bath. He's clearly trying to . get the **Waitress**'s

attention.

Waitress   Like, I'd love to send you a

Miranda   No.

I can't help.

No.

Once **Tommy** *and* **Johnny** *are in swimwear, they and*

Thomas *make their way towards the ice baths.*

.

The **Waitress** *leaves. She goes to* **Marlow, Jack**

and **Miranda** *watch.*

Marianne *gets onto all fours. She approaches the lunchbox*

as an animal. **Edmund** *watches.*

Waitress (*bit confused*)   Hi?

Marlow   Hi, how are you

Waitress   I'm good thank you, how are you

Marlow   I'm excellent, can I get a vodka and some ketamine.

Waitress (*looking around*)   Ummm, I'm not sure that that's my.

Marlow   Job?

Waitress   I guess so, yeah

Marlow   I mean, I can tell you it absolutely Is your job

Waitress   I mean

Marlow   I'm gonna give you ten thousand pounds.   .

And you're gonna go get me a bottle of vodka   .

She nudges at the lunchbox, manages to get it open, maybe she manages to eat a bit of the sandwich before she gives up, sits back on her knees and looks at **Edmund**, *upset.*

and a decent amount of ketamine and you can

keep whatever the change is okay?

.

Waitress   um

.

Marlow   Yes?

Waitress   .

Yes.

.

Marlow   .

.

Thank you?

Waitress   Thank you.

.

.

.

.

Marianne   I don't get it.   .

.

Edmund   It's not For you.

.

Marianne   Nothing's For Me.

Johnny and **Tommy** *head towards other ice baths/the
sauna.*

Marianne   The whole World's for you. And we just
have to fit in around the edges.

*She gets up and goes to start setting up microphones in
front of the ice baths/sauna, with the help of the* **Waitress**
when she's ready.

When **Edmund** *is on his own, he starts to eat the sandwich
and then lie on the floor, roll around.*

Marlow   Fuck off then.

She does. When she does, we're back in the podcast world. **Marianne** *and the* **Waitress** *spray the men with champagne. It's okay – good – if this is not beautifully choreographed, but messy and going a bit wrong.* **Edmund** *watches on, very alone.*

Joe   Holy shit

Johnny   ahhhhhhhhhhhhhhhhhhhhhhhhh

Joe   We're back we're ffffucking back on In   **Miranda** *and* **Jack** *are watching the podcast.*

Deep with the legend the man the OG the

Maestro and Patrick's new Fantasy Fuck

Marlow Roman and we are for some reason

Johnny   For some fucking reason

Joe   Up to our tits in a fucking ice bath

Patrick   You do this every day

Marlow   Fifteen Minutes twice a day

Joe   shiiiiit

Marlow   You not coming in?

Patrick You hear how steady his voice is

Marlow Ice bath, sauna, steam, it's all

Essential, guys

Patrick Get In, Patrick

Johnny No I mean.

No

Marlow No?

Patrick No

Marlow No?

Patrick No thank you

Marlow I'm not used to people saying No,

you scared DickFuck

Patrick No, I'm

I did mine earlier

Marlow BullShit

Joe Okay so this is a good moment – give us a .

blow by blow .

Johnny Straight up asking for a dick suck .

Joe Hey if I Had to ask a dude to suck my dick .

Patrick Couldn't pick a better guy .

At some point the **Waitress** *brings them some vodka and ketamine, but this goes unacknowledged – they just take it. She drops some off with* **Miranda** *and* **Jack** *too –* **Miranda** *partakes,* **Jack** *does not.*

Joe Give us – if you can – a little run-down of
your average day

As **Marlow** *runs through his day,* **Edmund** *starts to exercise.*

Marlow No day is average

Push-ups, skipping, weights – whatever.

Patrick For sure .

Marlow But Habits, routines can be helpful .

Joe Uh huh .

Marlow I'm up by 4 a.m. most days .

Joe   For real

Marlow   Weights, working out, a little cardio

Patrick   Uh huh

Marlow   I'm pushing myself, you know, and

my team – my whole, like

Wellness team

Joe   Uh huh

Johnny   THIS FEELS GENUINELY

INCREDIBLE

Marlow   They're looking at my data, my

numbers, heart rate, brainwaves, erections

Patrick   You serious

Marlow   You gotta get into Dick Health guys

Patrick   Okay I'm gonna be real with you

Marlow   Uh huh

Patrick   We've been doing this podcast for, what, like eight years

Joe   Yeah

Patrick   We've had some Stone Cold Legends on – no one as big as you but – fucking Dick Health? Never heard it before today

Marlow   Well, today's a new fucking day – you're not getting Hard at night you're gonna fucking die young – and not just cos my wife – who is a big Fan of my dick – would fucking kill me

Patrick   yeeeeeeeah

Marlow   Pipe down, you Pussy

Patrick   I'm just. I'm not a. Water creature I

Marlow   So my Team, yeah, my team they're

busy, right, they're making   . sure I'm eating
right, no dairy, no wheat, no sugar, no shit,
blood transfusions from my kids I mean we're
doing it right – I'm gonna live forever, boys,
don't die, you know?

Jack   I feel like I've not got long left.

Marianne (*into a microphone*)   I'm in a hotel
room with my legs spread and I'd love for you
to come and rearrange my insides.

Marlow   Don't die.

Waitress (*into a microphone*)   I've always just
felt like what I really want is to live on a farm
and raise eight children and milk cows and
bake bread and be a good wife to my husband,
support him however I can

Marlow   Don't die

.

I feel like death is coming

Joe   Don't die

Marianne (*into a microphone*)   I'm lying on a

bed with nothing on and I'm thinking about   .

you and your dick and you're lying next to

your wife who I know didn't fuck you tonight,   .

probably hasn't fucked you since

your honeymoon and when even was that and   .

(*is this the actor?*) is this what you want, is this

what I'm supposed to say

Marlow   Don't die

Marianne (*is this the actor?*)   Is that even my line .

Patrick   Don't die

Waitress   When I'm milking goats and my

eighth baby is latched onto my breast and I'm
wearing my gingham dress and I'm making a
blueberry pie and I'm digging up the potatoes
and I'm pouring my husband his beer and I'm
arranging the freshly cut wildflowers from our
field I feel so Alive (*is this the actor*) I'm sorry, I
can't, I'm not

Marianne   No that was good

Waitress   the bit with the goat is like

Marianne   no that was really convincing

Marlow   Don't die

Waitress   is that what they want

Marianne   yes I think that's what they want

Johnny   Don't die

Waitress   I *love* being a mother to all my

children but I do think there's something about   .

Mums and their boys   .

Marlow   Don't die

Marianne   I'm walking along a road and I've   .

just been to the supermarket and I bought   .

yoghurt and apples and a bottle of wine and a   .

car pulls up alongside me and a man leans out   .

of a window and says that he is a police officer   .

and shows me his badge and asks me to step   .

into the vehicle   .

Marlow   Don't die   .

Marianne   And I'm confused – that feels a bit –   .

is that what you   .

Johnny   Get into the car, please   .

Marianne   And he Is a police officer, he Is   .

showing me his badge and I feel a bit panicky a   .

bit like I want to call my Mum or my – can I call   .

my Mum   .

Patrick   Get into the car please   .

Marianne   And I haven't done anything wrong   .

so I   .

.   **Jack**   I feel like I am at the end

Ask again, is it okay if I just call my mum   .

Joe   Get into the car please   .

Waitress   I hold the baby and I pull on a   .

dress that has a bodice and I lean over a table –   .

is this what you want   .

Marianne   And so I get into the car and he's   .

only been driving for a minute before I realise   .

he is going to Kill me – is this what you want   .

Joe   Don't die.

Patrick   Don't die.

Marlow   Don't die.

Joe   Don't die.

Patrick   Don't die.

Marlow   Don't die

Joe   don't die.

Patrick   don't die.

Marlow   don't die.

Joe   don't die.

Patrick   don't die.

Marlow   don't die

Joe   don't die

Patrick   don't die

Marlow   don't die.

.

.

Miranda   Based on what.

A feeling?

Jack   Honestly. A bit.

.

I have seen So Much of it.

I have Watched so many people die.

Been sent out to Kill as many people as possible.

And then welcomed home but asked to

Shed that bit of ourselves, those extra layers of Skin

and Muscle and sinew and extra fucking Bile in my

guts or whatever it was that made me able to pull the

trigger so many fucking times and.

.

I don't know.

Having Seen so much of it, and been Responsible for so much of it I.

I can just feel it coming.

.

That and I can't stop falling over and when I cough there's blood.

.

Miranda   Okay, well.

Thank you for telling me.

.

I feel like my therapist would want to pass on her thanks.

.

Jack   Can I read you something.

Something I've been working on?

.

Miranda   No.

.

Jack   I Am sorry.

She looks at him.

She leaves. He nods. Everyone leaves. **Jack** *is on his own.*

Jack (*reading, to the audience, from a book*)   My father wanted only sons but he had to get through four dead daughters before he got to the sons, but at least the sons lived.

Part Five

IS THIS WINTER?

Jack *is standing outside his childhood home. He looks unwell. It's boiling hot. He's waiting.* **Edmund** *approaches, but remains at a distance.* **Marlow** *steps out of the house.*

A little time passes. **Jack** *nods.*

Jack   Thank you for coming.

.

Marlow   I haven't been here since I was a boy.

.

Jack   Did you want to look inside?

.

Edmund *shakes his head.*

Edmund   I can't go back in there.

.

I can't really go inside anywhere but I'm pretty sure if I stepped into that house I'd die.

.

I have to stay back, is that okay?

.

They nod.

Marlow   You didn't get enough for it, it's a pretty sort of weekend pile

Jack   It's a ruin

Marlow   History though, people love history, could've sold it to a gullible Yank

Jack   It has Misery crawling all over it I don't know why I ever thought I could make it something else.

.

I wish.

I wish we had some Shared Memory. Just one.

.

Some game or mischief or even that we had had the opportunity to Be together in grief but.

.

I do not know either of you.

And I am sorry for it.

.

And.

Perhaps I am grateful for it too, I.

.

It is so hot for December.

Marlow   Not as hot as last year's. It is over-exaggerated. Hysteria whipped up by a mainstream media.

Edmund   The world is on fire.

Marlow   Forgive me if I do not take the local Whackjob as a reliable source

Edmund   Who bought the house

Jack   A developer. He's going to bulldoze it. Build a block of flats with a swimming pool in the basement and a sky garden.

Edmund   Oh.

Marlow   Good.

Jack   Is it?

Marlow   We can't stand still. We have to Move.

Jack   I.

.

I.

.

Is there Anything we could do to

Mark this.

Anything that might Unite us.

A prayer for Mother, a word for Father.

.

Is there Anything that might unite us.

.

Is there Anything that we could Do that might suggest that there is yet hope.

That any of it was worth it.

.

Is there anything at all.

.

Anything at all.

.

The light, very slowly, fades to black.

Discover. Read. Listen. Watch.

A NEW WAY TO ENGAGE WITH PLAYS

This award-winning digital library features over 3,000 playtexts, 400 audio plays, 300 hours of video and 360 scholarly books.

Playtexts published by Methuen Drama, The Arden Shakespeare, Faber & Faber, Playwrights Canada Press, Aurora Metro Books and Nick Hern Books.

Audio Plays from L.A. Theatre Works featuring classic and modern works from the oeuvres of leading American playwrights.

Video collections including films of live performances from the RSC, The Globe and The National Theatre, as well as acting masterclasses and BBC feature films and documentaries.

FIND OUT MORE:
www.dramaonlinelibrary.com • @dramaonlinelib

For a complete listing of
Methuen Drama titles, visit:

www.bloomsbury.com/drama

Follow us on X and keep up to date with
our news and publications

@MethuenDrama